Contents

Chapter One:
1974–1980

Derek's Dream

Derek Jeter had a dream.

When he was a young boy, all Derek Jeter wanted to do when he grew up was play shortstop for the New York Yankees, his favorite team. Every night before he went to sleep, he would lay in his bed and imagine that he was on the infield at Yankee Stadium, scooping up ground balls and throwing runners out at first, turning game-ending double plays, or smacking the winning hit in the World Series.

In school Derek would write book reports and other assignments about the Yankees. Whenever his teachers asked him what he wanted to be, he answered simply, "I'm going to play shortstop for the New York Yankees." As Derek once told a reporter, they'd usually laugh and tell his parents, "You shouldn't put those ideas in your son's head."

Most kids have dreams similar to Derek's. But just dreaming about doing something doesn't mean it's going to happen. The odds against such dreams coming true are astronomical.

At any given moment there are only about five thousand players in professional baseball, less than a thousand in the major leagues. Each team in the majors, like the Yankees, has only twenty-five players. And of those twenty-five, usually only one or two play shortstop.

Yet Derek was able to make his dream come true despite these nearly insurmountable odds. His parents taught Derek that the only way to make dreams come true is to work hard for them; and then, when they do come true, to keep on working hard. Those values have helped make Derek Jeter one of the greatest players in baseball, and one of the most popular. Today, he is the shortstop for the New York Yankees. His boyhood dream has come true.

Since first joining the Yankees starting lineup in 1996, Derek Jeter has helped the New York team win four world championships and six pennants. He is considered one of baseball's greatest players and has a chance to become one of the all-time greats.

He is also one of the most popular players in the game, sometimes admired as much for his good looks and effervescent personality as for his athletic talents.

"I'm living a dream," he once admitted to a reporter. "If that's the case, I don't ever want anyone to wake me up."

Derek's dream started about twenty-five miles west of Yankee Stadium in Pequannock, New Jersey, where he was born on June 26, 1974, the first child of Charles and Dorothy Jeter.

Derek's father, Charles, had attended Fisk University in Tennessee on an academic scholarship. In order to maintain his scholarship, Charles had to put his studies first. But sports were also important to Charles, as they were to his entire family. Two of his relatives, including defensive lineman Gary Jeter, found careers in professional football.

Despite his academic schedule, Charles still found time to play shortstop on the school team. Although he was a very good baseball player, he wasn't quite talented enough to play professionally. After graduating with a degree in business administration, he entered the military service.

While stationed in Germany, he met a young woman in the military named Dorothy Connors. They started dating, fell in love, and got married.

There was just one problem. Charles Jeter was African-American. Dorothy Connors was white. This was during the late 1960s, when marriages between people of different races were rare. Such couples often encountered prejudice from those who thought that it was wrong for people of different races to marry one another. In some states, it was even illegal!

But Charles and Dorothy didn't allow that to stop them. They loved each other and were determined to make their marriage work. They returned to the United States and settled in New Jersey, near Dorothy's family. A short while later Derek was born.

Derek was a precocious young child and his parents doted on him, as did his many relatives. He was fortunate to grow up in such a warm and supportive environment. Derek has told reporters, "I'll brag about my family all day long."

In 1979, when Derek was five years old, Dorothy Jeter had another child, a girl the Jeters named

Sharlee. With a growing family, Charles Jeter decided to return to college.

He moved the family to Kalamazoo, Michigan, a small but vibrant city, and enrolled in Western Michigan University. Dorothy Jeter, who worked as an accountant, was able to get a transfer.

Although Derek's parents were often busy, they successfully juggled the demands of school and work to take care of their children. After Charles Jeter received his master's degree, he went on to get a doctorate.

Thanks to Charles, five-year-old Derek already loved baseball. Whenever Charles had the chance, he played pickup softball in the neighborhood. Derek loved watching his father glide across the ground to field the ball or get a hit and run around the bases. He wanted to be just like him and peppered his father with questions about baseball.

Sometimes he would sit in Charles' lap and look at his father's scrapbook about his collegiate baseball career. Over and over again, Derek would ask his father to tell him about his best game and the biggest hit he ever had. Just over the fence in the backyard of their home was the baseball field for Kalamazoo Central High School. Derek loved scrambling over the fence to play catch with his father on the diamond.

Every summer they all returned to New Jersey to visit with relatives. When his parents returned to Michigan, Derek sometimes stayed behind for a few weeks with his grandparents, Dot and Bill "Sonny" Connors, and some of his cousins. Other than his parents, Dot and Sonny were the two most important people in his life.

Most mornings, Sonny Connors was already gone when Derek woke up. Sonny was the head of maintenance for a large church and had to be at work at six-thirty in the morning. He never missed a day, not even when he felt sick. Everyone who knew him liked him. "That's a lesson I learned from him," Derek once told a reporter. "He didn't make millions, but he affected many lives."

While his grandfather worked, Derek spent time with his grandmother. Dot Connors absolutely loved baseball, particularly the New York Yankees. She'd been a Yankee fan since she was a young girl, and she told Derek stories about some of the great Yankee players of the past, like Babe Ruth, perhaps the greatest slugger ever, or graceful outfielder Joe DiMaggio. At night, he'd sit with his grandparents and watch the Yankees play on television, often falling asleep in their arms.

As soon as he woke up each morning he'd run to wake his grandmother. "All his cousins would still be sleeping," Derek's grandmother once told a reporter, "and Derek would say, 'Come on, Gram! Let's throw!'"

Confronted with such enthusiasm, Dot Connors would laugh and soon follow her grandson outside. They'd spend hours throwing the ball back and forth. Even then he had a strong arm. Dot Connors recalls that his throws would almost knock her over.

When Derek was six years old, Dot took him to Yankee Stadium to see the Yankees for the first time. He couldn't believe how big the Stadium was or how green the grass was. He loved seeing the Yankees play.

Over the years Derek and his grandmother made many more trips to Yankee Stadium. Dot Connors bought Derek Yankee hats and Yankee shirts, and he would proudly put them on before going to the

Stadium. He would even bring his glove along in case a ball was hit his direction. After the game Dot Connors would take Derek outside the Stadium to the players' entrance and wait patiently while Derek got the autographs of his favorite players, like star outfielder Dave Winfield.

This is when Derek Jeter began to dream. He wanted to play shortstop, like his father, and he wanted to play for the Yankees, his favorite team. Playing shortstop for the New York Yankees would be a dream come true.

Although adults sometimes scoff at the dreams of young children, Derek's family took him seriously. His mother once told a reporter, "We've always told our kids they could be better than anybody else." When Derek told his father about his dream, Charles Jeter calmly explained to Derek that the only way to make his dream come true would be to try very hard and practice for hours.

"If you are dedicated and you work hard," he said, "all your dreams will come true."

Derek Jeter has never forgotten those words.

Chapter Two:
1981–1989

From T-ball to Prospect

When Derek was six years old he began attending St. Augustine's grammar school, a private Catholic school in Kalamazoo. Like most parents, the Jeters were a little worried about their son on the first day of school. But their concerns went beyond the normal anxiety a parent feels as a child grows up.

Derek was of mixed race, part African-American and part white. Although the Jeters had taught Derek that racial differences didn't matter and that all people should be treated equally, they knew that not everyone was so open-minded. They worried that once Derek started school he would be exposed to children who may have adopted their parents' prejudices. Even though the schools in Kalamazoo were well integrated, children sometimes picked on those they perceived as being different, and Derek was different from many of his classmates. His parents were concerned that some black children might tease Derek about being white, and that some white kids would taunt him about being black.

But the Jeters had prepared their son well. Derek had a great personality and a quick smile. He treated everyone with respect and was able to make friends with everybody, regardless of ethnicity. In fact, Derek's racial heritage has never caused him a problem. He considers it an advantage. He once told a reporter, "No one knows what I am. I can relate to everyone. I've got all kinds of friends."

Derek's parents always emphasized the importance of education to their children. "First of all," his father has said, "we want them to do well academically." They made it clear to Derek that school was more important than any after-school activity, even baseball. In fact, they used Derek's love of sports to help motivate him.

At the beginning of every school year they sat with their son and wrote out a contract. "The contract outlined study hours, curfews, and participation in school activities," said Charles Jeter. Derek and his parents would discuss his goals and the things he hoped to do away from school, like play sports and hang out with his friends. Then Derek and his parents would all sign the contract. If Derek fulfilled his part of the contract, his parents would allow him to do the things he hoped to do.

Baseball soon became the focus of almost everything Derek wanted to do. Like many little boys, he started out playing T-ball before moving up to Little League when he was ten years old.

Derek was a star from the very beginning. All the time he'd spent playing catch with his father and his grandmother had given him a very strong arm. He took the game much more seriously than most boys his age did.

Derek's father told him exactly what he would have to do in order to fulfill his dream. Charles didn't ever want his son simply to depend on the fact that he was more talented than other boys his age. He explained to Derek that there would always be someone, somewhere, with more talent. Derek later told a reporter, "My folks taught me that there may be people who have more talent, but there's never any excuse for anyone to work harder than you do — and I believe that."

Charles Jeter also tried to make his son understand what it was like to compete. When he played with Derek, whether it was a game of checkers or a game of basketball, he never let up to allow Derek to win. Instead, he showed his son what he would have to do to win on his own.

When Derek moved up to Little League, his father served as his coach. Although Derek had played shortstop in T-ball, at their first practice, his father told him to play second base. At first, Derek didn't understand.

But Charles Jeter knew what he was doing. He wanted to teach Derek not to take anything for granted in baseball. He would have to earn his position just like everyone else on the team.

Derek learned his lesson well. He played second as well as he could, and by the middle of the season he had played his way into the starting shortstop position.

Already, people around Kalamazoo were talking about the great young baseball player named Jeter who was tearing up Little League. Yet as good as Derek was, his father patiently explained that he had to be even better if he hoped to achieve his dream.

"I wanted Derek to be an all-around player," Charles Jeter explained years later. He told Derek that if he really wanted to play shortstop for the Yankees, being the best player in his league or even the best player in Kalamazoo wouldn't be enough. He would have to try to be better. His mother recalled, "My husband always told Derek to compare himself with the kids who really wanted to play ball."

Part of becoming the best player he could be was learning to control his emotions. During one Little League game Derek came to bat against one of the best pitchers in the league.

As the first pitch came in, Derek swung as hard as he could.

Whiff! "Strike one!" said the umpire.

Then the pitcher threw another one down the middle.

Whiff! Derek swung through the pitch for strike two.

Angry at missing the first two pitches, he told himself to be more patient. The pitcher wound up and threw, and Derek watched the pitch pass by, certain it was a ball.

"Strike three!" the umpire called. "You're out!"

Derek couldn't believe it. He hardly ever struck out. He stormed back to the bench and complained loudly about the umpire, telling his father, "It's a bad call!"

Charles Jeter watched his young son continue to rant and rave for a few minutes, then stopped him. "You just swung at the two pitches before," he said calmly. "Why would you complain about the umpire? Control what you can control."

Derek immediately realized that he was wrong. He shouldn't have been angry with the umpire. He should have been angry at himself for swinging and missing at two pitches and putting himself at a disadvantage. The incident made an impression on Derek, and he has since told the story many times.

In the evenings, after his team had finished playing, Derek, his parents, and his sister, Sharlee, would often hop the fence of the high school field to play some more. Derek has recalled, "I would go out and Dad would hit me a lot of grounders," most of them almost out of his reach, so Derek could increase his range. Charles taught Derek how to move his feet to keep his balance and to throw the ball quickly and accurately. Then Derek would practice hitting as his father threw batting practice. "My mom and sister would be in the outfield and would flag down all the balls I would hit," he remembers.

But practice wasn't focused entirely on Derek. Sharlee always got to take a turn hitting and fielding, too, and Derek had to chase down her hits. She later became a star softball player who Derek once described as "a better shortstop than I am."

The Jeters never had to force Derek to practice, and they never pressured him to play. Charles Jeter had earned his doctorate degree in psychology and he knew that if he tried to force Derek to do anything it might backfire. He simply asked Derek what he wanted to accomplish and then provided Derek with a strategy to make those dreams come true. The rest was up to Derek.

Although Derek's Little League teams weren't very good, he was among the best players in the league. When he turned thirteen years old, Derek moved up to Mickey Mantle League.

Even though he was competing against older

players, Derek was still one of the best players in the league. His team had an established shortstop, so Derek played third base. Although he was unfamiliar with the position, all the time he'd spent practicing had helped develop the all-around skills he needed to succeed.

Derek would have played baseball every day if he'd had the chance. But the winters are cold and snowy in Michigan, so in the fall and winter Derek played basketball. He gave the game almost as much attention as he did baseball in the spring and summer, even attending basketball camp at the University of Michigan. He loved playing and he knew that basketball could only help him become a better baseball player.

Playing shortstop for the Yankees was still his dream. That was all he talked about. In eighth grade his English teacher gave everyone an assignment to write a story about what they wanted to be. Derek, naturally, wrote about playing shortstop for the Yankees in the World Series. In his eighth-grade yearbook his classmates described him as "most likely to play shortstop for the New York Yankees."

After graduating from eighth grade, Derek enrolled at Kalamazoo Central High School. He could hardly wait for baseball season to begin.

Tryouts for the baseball team began in March. As a ninth grader, Derek knew that it would be virtually impossible for him to make the varsity team. The varsity shortstop was a senior who had already earned all-conference honors. Derek just hoped to make the junior varsity. The coaches had already heard about Derek and were anxious to see him play.

The first practice took place in the school gym because it was still too wet and cold to play outside. After warming up, the coaches had the players line up and hit them ground balls. When it was Derek's turn he expertly fielded the skipping ball, set himself, and threw the ball to another player across the gym.

Thwack! The ball smacked into the player's mitt and the sound echoed throughout the gym.

Junior varsity coach Norman Copeland's eyes grew very wide. "I knew I wouldn't be able to keep him on the junior varsity for long," he said later. Derek already looked like a ballplayer. For his age, he was tall, rangy, and fast. His bat was quick and he worked harder than anyone else on the team. When his coaches told him something, he got it right the very first time.

Derek began the season as the starting junior varsity shortstop. He impressed everyone with his play, even the opposition. In one game, he took three relay throws from the outfield and threw out three runners at home plate!

Observers were just as impressed with Jeter's attitude. Many accomplished young athletes get big heads. But Derek rarely talked about himself or his achievements. He was only concerned about his team. And in class he didn't act like a big jock. He still studied hard and treated everyone with respect.

Halfway through the season it became clear to Derek's coaches that he wasn't just the best player on the junior varsity; he was probably the best player in the whole school. Even the starting varsity shortstop realized that Derek was better. Near the end of the season he magnanimously offered to move to third base so Derek could play shortstop for the varsity. Although Derek wasn't quite as dominant on the varsity as he had been on the JV squad, he wasn't overmatched.

When the high school season ended Derek joined the Connie Mack League. Despite being one of the youngest players in the league, he wanted to try out for the Kalamazoo Maroons, a team made up of the best Connie Mack players in the city. They played an ambitious schedule all over the state.

Charles Jeter encouraged him to try out for the team. "He told me not to be disappointed if I didn't start," Derek said later. "He said I could learn from the player I played behind." Derek made the team and was soon starting.

As Derek's high school coach Don Zomer recalled, even though he was playing with older kids, Derek stood out. "It was so obvious," he said.

The team played a grueling schedule of 65 to 70 games. "Every day except for travel," Jeter remembers. Playing for the Maroons against many of the best high school players in Michigan helped Derek improve rapidly. As he recalled later, he hit about .340 in his first season with the Maroons. He soon began to be noticed by professional baseball scouts.

Big league baseball teams are always looking for talent. Each year they have a draft of amateur players. They employ scouts who attend hundreds of games each year looking for prospects. Although teams are not allowed to draft players until after they have finished high school, they start looking at them when they are only fourteen or fifteen years old.

At many of the Maroons' games, Derek and his teammates would notice the scouts. They usually sat together behind the backstop with radar guns to time the speed of pitches and pads of paper to take notes about the players they were watching.

Derek hoped they were starting to take some notes about him.

Chapter Three:
1989-1991

Draft Pick Dream

When Derek started his sophomore year of high school, he already stood over six feet tall. He was nearly as talented on the basketball court as he was on the baseball diamond. He played for the high school varsity and on an AAU team with future University of Michigan and NBA stars Chris Webber and Jalen Rose.

But baseball was still Jeter's favorite. In the spring he could hardly wait for baseball season to begin. He again played shortstop for the varsity, and even though he was only a sophomore, he was one of the team leaders. Derek was usually the first player on the practice field and the last player off. During games he was constantly shouting words of encouragement to his teammates and doing whatever he could to help his team win.

21

When he joined the Maroons for another season of summer baseball, he had improved tremendously. Not only was he the best player on his team — he was clearly one of the best players in the state. He was improving both at bat and in the field, lifting his average and being much more consistent defensively.

Yet Derek wasn't satisfied. He worried that because the Maroons played games so often he wasn't getting enough time to practice. So Derek started showing up an hour early just so he could practice fielding ground balls.

But Maroons coach Mike Hinga was more impressed with the way Derek behaved than he was with how he played. Even though he was the top player on the team, he worked harder than anyone else and was never arrogant or self-centered. Team goals were always more important to Derek than his individual accomplishments. Hinga summed him up simply, telling a reporter, "He's sincere."

When baseball season began in Derek's junior year of high school, the baseball scouts started following him in earnest. He had gotten their attention with the Maroons, and now they started watching him closely.

But professional scouts weren't the only people interested in Derek's future. Colleges from all around the country also coveted Derek. He was a rare commodity, for not only was he a great player, he was a great student, too. Every day in the mail he received all sorts of college catalogs.

Faced with so much scrutiny, some young players get nervous and start to press. But Derek just kept getting better. He flourished during his junior year, hitting an incredible .557, a school record, with 34 RBIs and 22 stolen bases. He only struck out one time.

He was just as impressive in the field. He was so quick and his arm was so strong that Derek played shortstop while standing in short left field!

His reputation soon began to spread. Reporters for national publications like *Baseball America*, which covers high school and college baseball, started writing about the young prospect from Kalamazoo. Observers began predicting that after his senior season Derek would be one of the top draft picks in the nation.

But while everyone else was worried about his future, all Derek wanted to do was enjoy his senior year of high school. Although he hoped to be drafted by a professional team, Derek knew that the chances for a career in pro baseball were still slim. His mother later told a reporter, "We told him if he worked hard he'd have options. Right now, he has options."

Derek's scores on the ACT and SAT, special tests taken before college, were excellent, and his grades were among the top ten percent in his class. He was a member of the National Honor Society and the president of the school's Latin club. He did well in all his classes, but particularly liked math. His father described him as a "serious student." Derek told people that if a career in baseball didn't work out, he wanted to become a doctor.

His academic performance combined with his athletic prowess made him very attractive to colleges. Dozens of schools offered him scholarships to play baseball in the event he decided not to play professionally right out of high school.

Although he was recruited by some of the biggest baseball schools in the country, like the University of Florida, Derek wasn't sure he wanted to go so far from home.

The University of Michigan was also interested in

Derek. Michigan had a good academic reputation, and baseball coach Bill Freehan, a former star catcher with the Detroit Tigers, was well respected. Jeter had visited the school several times and had come away impressed.

Freehan called Jeter "the best player I've ever seen [in high school]," but he was just as impressed by Derek Jeter the person. "Derek's an outstanding young man," he told a reporter. "You can tell that by the way he conducts himself. He's the type of young man you want in your program." Even though he knew that there was a good chance Derek would be drafted after high school and turn pro, he still offered Derek a scholarship.

That fall, Derek accepted the scholarship offer from Michigan. Both Derek and his parents recognized that education was important, and if he wasn't drafted or didn't feel comfortable turning pro, playing baseball while attending the University of Michigan could still help him fulfill his dream.

Derek's final year of high school passed in a blur. He enjoyed playing his final season of basketball, and was captain of the team. But he could hardly wait for baseball season to start.

When Kalamazoo started their season in early April, it was still cold. But that didn't prevent the professional scouts from turning out to see Derek play. For the first few games of the season more than forty scouts were in attendance.

Derek didn't disappoint them. Strong and quick, he now stood six foot three and weighed one hundred seventy pounds. His coach, Don Zomer, gave Derek a glowing scouting report of his own, telling a reporter, "He has good foot speed, he hits well, and he hits with power. He's got a gun for an arm. . . . He's got it all, and I still say he's a better person than a baseball player."

In fact, Derek's arm was so strong that Zomer had to replace his first baseman. The pro scouts were timing Derek's throws from shortstop at ninety-one miles per hour, and Central's first baseman simply couldn't handle them.

Derek got off to a flying start in his final season of high school baseball. In his first seven at bats, he hit three home runs!

The scouts were thrilled. When they look at players, they evaluate them in five categories, or tools —

hitting, fielding, throwing, running, and hitting for power. Derek had already displayed the ability to hit, field, throw, and run. But now he was hitting for power, too. Players with all five tools are very rare.

Derek's stock in the upcoming draft rose dramatically. He was now considered one of the best high school players in the country. Some people even expected him to be the first pick in the entire draft.

But on one snowy, early-spring afternoon, Derek hit a ground ball and ran hard to first base. As he crossed the base his foot slipped on the wet bag.

Derek flew though the air and landed heavily on the ground. He felt a sharp pain in his ankle.

He sat on the ground in agony, unable to stand. He was afraid his ankle was broken. He knew that if it was, the pro scouts might lose interest in him. A broken ankle can take a long time to heal.

Derek's family rushed him to the hospital for x-rays. Time seemed to stop while he waited for the results. All of a sudden his dream of playing shortstop for the Yankees seemed just that — a dream.

Then the doctor came back after looking at the x-rays and gave Derek some good news. His ankle wasn't broken. He just had a bad sprain. Derek let out a big sigh of relief, then started worrying again. Even an ankle sprain can take a long time to heal.

The injury taught him a valuable lesson. He learned not to take his talent for granted. He knew that everything could change in an instant.

But over the next week his ankle slowly started feeling better. Still, he was forced to miss three games. When he did return to the lineup, it was hard to run. He served as designated hitter for several games until the ankle healed.

Even though the ankle wasn't one hundred percent, Derek insisted on playing in the field again. He knew that he had to prove to the scouts that he was healthy.

He needn't have worried. Even though his ankle was sore he continued to play spectacularly. The only lingering effect of the injury came at the plate. He had a hard time turning on the ankle, and for the remainder of the year he hit only one more home run.

Fortunately, the scouts understood. If anything, his determination impressed them even more. Despite the injury and the fact that the opposition rarely gave him any good pitches to hit, he still collected 30 hits in 59 at bats for an average of .508, with five doubles, one triple, four home runs, 12 stolen bases, and 25 RBIs.

As draft day approached, Derek started to get nervous. *Baseball America* had named him High School Player of the Year, as had the American Baseball Coaches Association. He was also named to *USA Today*'s high school all-star team. He was certain to be one of the first players chosen in the draft.

The *Kalamazoo Gazette* reported that the Houston Astros would select Derek with the first pick in the draft. Others believed that Cincinnati, with the fifth pick in the draft, would be certain to pick him.

Derek was excited, but also a little worried. Over the course of the season he had met with scouts from every major league team except one. The only team that hadn't contacted Derek was the team with the sixth pick in the draft, the New York Yankees. They didn't seem interested. Derek was disappointed, but he knew there was nothing he could do about it. Teams had to draft players according to their needs.

The Yankees needed a catcher, and most people expected them to select Charles Johnson, the All-American catcher from the University of Miami.

But just two days before the draft, a scout named Dick Groch called the Jeters and introduced himself. He told them he hadn't contacted them earlier because he didn't want to intrude. He explained that he'd been watching Derek for the past two years, and just wanted to make sure that Derek was still interested in playing professionally. Teams don't want to waste a draft pick on a player who intends to go to college.

There was nothing unique about the call. But when Groch said he was a scout for the New York Yankees, Derek's heart leaped into his throat.

Groch was noncommittal. He didn't promise Derek that the Yankees would draft him. He just told him that he was among the players they were considering.

The draft was scheduled to begin at 1:00 P.M. on June 1, 1992. Derek went to bed the night before nervous with anticipation.

"I didn't get to sleep until four A.M.," he said later.

"I kept thinking about what would happen if I started slipping."

Unlike the professional football or basketball drafts, the major league baseball draft isn't televised or broadcast on radio. Derek and his family had to wait for a phone call to learn of his fate.

Every time the phone rang that afternoon, Derek jumped. His mother would answer and Derek would look at her expectantly, but time after time it was only one of Derek's friends or relatives calling to ask if he'd been drafted yet.

Then the phone rang again. His mother answered it, listened for a moment, and turned to Derek with a big smile on her face and handed him the phone.

"It's the Yankees," she said.

Derek's dream was in sight.

Chapter Four:
1991-1993

Strides Toward Success

That one phone call changed Derek's life. He spoke to Yankee general manager Gene Michael for a few moments. Michael congratulated him and told him the Yankees would be in touch in another few days to discuss a contract. Then the family began to celebrate.

Within minutes the local press began to gather at his house. Derek was so happy he hardly knew what to say.

"I knew I was projected to go to Cincinnati," he said. "And I knew the Yankees picked next. I can't explain how I feel. They have a great tradition and a great team. Everything is just great in New York. I couldn't believe they drafted me."

His mother shared his joy. "It's just amazing," she said. "I grew up a Yankees fan."

Over the next few weeks Derek's father and an adviser negotiated with the Yankees by phone. Meanwhile, Derek went back to playing baseball with the Maroons.

On June 26, Derek turned eighteen years old, and his father thought it was time to negotiate with the Yankees in person. Scout Dick Groch and several other Yankees representatives came to Kalamazoo.

The Yankees offered Derek a contract worth $800,000, including a bonus of $700,000, a very good proposal. But Derek's father insisted that the Yankees pay for Derek's college education no matter how well he did in professional baseball. The Yankees readily agreed.

On June 28, Derek signed the contract. He was a professional baseball player.

Two days later he got on a plane, left his family behind, and traveled to Tampa, Florida, site of the Yankees' minor league training camp and home of their rookie league team in the Gulf Coast League.

Historically, the New York Yankees are the most successful franchise in professional sports. Since winning their first American League pennant in 1921, the Yankees had captured another thirty-two league titles. And in thirty-three World Series, the Yankees had won a record twenty-two times.

Ever since the Yankees had acquired slugger Babe Ruth in 1920, many of the best players in the game had worn the famous pinstriped uniform of the Yankees, including such Hall-of-Famers as first baseman Lou Gehrig, catcher Bill Dickey, outfielders Joe DiMaggio, Mickey Mantle, and Reggie Jackson, and pitchers Whitey Ford and Catfish Hunter. Those were the Yankees Derek's grandmother had told him about and the reason he had become a Yankees fan.

But in recent years the Yankees had fallen on hard times. They hadn't played in the postseason since winning the pennant in 1981, and hadn't won the World Series since 1978.

They'd played particularly poorly in recent years, finishing with records under .500. One of the reasons for that was their farm system. The Yankees simply hadn't been very good at drafting and developing good young players. And on the rare occasions they did, they were often impatient, either rushing them to the major leagues before they were ready or trading them away for more established players, most of whom played poorly for New York. The team was in a rut.

New York's selection of Jeter, the first high school player picked in the 1992 draft, was significant.

High school players generally take a long time to develop. Drafting Jeter appeared to indicate that the Yankees were changing their strategy and planned to rebuild with younger players.

Even though the Yankees told Jeter and his parents they had no intention of rushing him to the major leagues, Derek was under a great deal of pressure. From the day he signed his contract, Yankees fans and team officials expected Derek Jeter to one day lead the franchise back to glory.

That was a lot to expect from a player who had just turned eighteen years old. For even though Jeter had been dreaming of becoming a professional baseball player for his entire life and his father and coaches had done their best to make sure he was ready, there was no real way to prepare him for everything he would face in pro ball. Derek would have to grow up fast.

For the first time in his life he had to learn to live on his own. Except to stay with his grandmother in New Jersey, Jeter had never been away from home before. He later described the experience of moving to Florida from Michigan as like "going to another country."

At the same time he had to make the adjustment to professional baseball. For years, Derek had been the top player on the field. Now he was just another player. Even though rookie league baseball is for players in their first or second year of pro baseball, they were still the best players Derek had ever played with or against. And Derek was one of the youngest players in the league. Many players were three or four years older than he was.

Only two days after arriving in Tampa, Derek played his first professional games. It was a humbling experience. In a doubleheader he came to bat seven times and didn't get a single hit. He couldn't even remember the last time he'd gone seven at bats without a hit. He quickly discovered that he still had a lot to learn about baseball, and went another eight at bats before he got his first professional hit.

He also learned that there was a big difference between playing baseball and working baseball. In Tampa, Jeter and his teammates spent all morning working out and practicing, then all afternoon in the hot Florida sun playing games. At the end of the day he was exhausted.

He was also miserable. Derek recalled later, "I

didn't have any fun. I was worried about how I played. I was homesick. I wanted to go home when I got there. When I went to bat I'd be thinking about how many days I had left before I could go home." Within a few days he began to question his own abilities, later admitting, "I was thinking I should have gone to school." Every evening, he called home.

When the phone rang in the Jeter house, his parents would look at one another, knowing that Derek was on the line. They'd take turns answering the phone to talk to their son.

They would listen patiently as Jeter described the difficulties he was having, then try to restore his confidence. Charles Jeter kept telling his son not to dwell on his mistakes but to try to improve the next time. They talked so long and so often that Derek ran up phone bills of up to four hundred dollars per month. The Yankees even flew the Jeters to Tampa once to keep their son company.

The Yankees kept their promise not to rush him. During his first season of professional baseball, the Yankees professed not to really care how well he played. They just wanted him to get accustomed to the routines of professional baseball. They were cautious and didn't want to overwhelm him. In fact, they gave him very little instruction at all.

Jeter didn't play very well and was a little confused by the way the Yankees reacted. No matter how poorly he played, neither manager Gary Denbo nor anyone else on the Yankee staff seemed upset. They told the press that they were pleased with the way he played, but some observers began writing that Jeter was a flop and questioned his future.

And Jeter did play poorly, particularly at the plate. After using aluminum bats in amateur baseball, Jeter had to adjust to hitting with wood bats, which is much more difficult. He was also overmatched by many of the pitchers he faced. He hit for little power and had more strikeouts than base hits. He finished the year with a batting average of only .202.

He did a little better in the field, committing only 12 errors in 47 games, but he was terribly inconsistent and often struggled badly during practice.

When the rookie league season ended in late summer of 1992, the Yankees had Derek report to their single-A minor league team in Greensboro, North Carolina, for the balance of the season. Although there were only a couple of weeks left, they were thinking about sending Derek to Greensboro in 1993 and wanted him to feel comfortable there.

Although Derek still struggled in the field, he did hit a bit better. Manager Trey Hillman immediately saw that Jeter had tremendous potential, but was still raw. He began working with Derek to help make him more consistent.

When the season ended, the Yankees gave him a treat. They brought him to New York, where he got to watch a few games in Yankee Stadium and meet some of the current Yankees, like star first baseman Don Mattingly. Although Jeter had been to Yankee Stadium dozens of times before, being able to see it from the field was an entirely new experience. He was thrilled.

Still, after the trip to New York, Jeter was delighted to return to Michigan. When he did, he enrolled at the University of Michigan and moved to nearby Ann Arbor. Although he wasn't eligible to play college baseball, he was eager to begin his education.

He took classes, primarily in business, and lived like a college student. He was able to visit his parents whenever he wanted, and finally got accustomed to living on his own.

He was also able to put his first season of professional baseball in perspective. He realized that his experience wasn't unique. Lots of players, even great players, struggle in their first season.

But before Jeter completed the fall semester, the Yankees asked him to return to Florida and play in the instructional league. With his new attitude about his first season, Derek agreed readily. Though he was enjoying college life at U of M, he wasn't ready to give up on his dream just yet, and was glad the Yankees weren't either.

The instructional league is just what it appears to be — a league in which the focus is on instruction. Just like rookie league, players practice in the morning and then play in the afternoon. Jeter thrived in this new environment. He felt much more confident and assured than he had in the summer.

The New York coaching staff began working with Jeter, gradually making changes in the way he hit and fielded to help him become more consistent. Ever so slowly, he began to improve.

The Yankees invited Jeter to attend spring training with the major league team in 1993. They wanted him to see what it would take to become a major league ballplayer.

When Jeter arrived at camp in Fort Lauderdale in March of 1993, he was a different player than he had been the year before, much more confident and self-assured. The extra instruction he had received helped, but so did the fact that he was a year older and bet-ter prepared for living the baseball player's life.

Jeter loved being at training camp, where he was able to watch major leaguers hit and field up close for the first time. New York manager Buck Showal-ter even surprised Jeter by playing him in a couple of exhibition games. The Yankees made it clear that they still thought he'd become a great player. Infield coach Clete Boyer described him as "like a little colt" and said, "He's got raw ability."

But perhaps the most important thing he learned at training camp was how to act and behave like a big leaguer. For the first time, he realized that the biggest difference between a big leaguer and other professional ballplayers was the amount of work they did and how seriously they took baseball. He couldn't believe how hard some of the Yankees worked.

Late one afternoon, finally finished with practice, Jeter stayed on the field until virtually everyone was gone except the Yankee captain, veteran first baseman Don Mattingly. The former MVP, batting champion, and All-Star was getting in some extra work on his own.

Jeter watched Mattingly working out and marveled over the fact that the star slugger was the hardest worker in camp. Then Jeter started to trudge in toward the clubhouse, exhausted after a long day working in the hot sun. As he slowly walked in, Mattingly jogged up to him and tapped him on the shoulder.

"We'd better run in," he told Jeter. "You never know who's watching." Then Mattingly took off.

Jeter was startled. He could hardly believe that a big star like Don Mattingly cared enough to speak with him and give him some advice. Jeter then broke into a sprint and caught up with Mattingly, and the two players raced together toward the clubhouse.

With each stride he took, Derek Jeter was taking a big step toward fulfilling his dream.

Chapter Five:
1993–1995

Hits and Misses

In mid-March the Yankees sent Jeter to their minor league camp. He had learned as much as he could hanging around major leaguers. Now it was time to work on his game again.

At the end of camp, as Jeter had expected, the Yankees assigned him to their single-A team in the South Atlantic League in Greensboro, North Carolina. There, his rapid improvement continued. As Jeter later told a reporter, he was able to relax, saying, "When you play one hundred forty games there will always be another game tomorrow, so I try to make it fun."

Jeter finally began making the adjustments necessary to succeed in professional baseball, particularly at the plate. Like many high school stars, Jeter had been a power hitter. But in pro ball, he was sometimes overmatched and had a hard time getting around on fastballs on the inside half of the plate. He had to learn to adjust and stop trying to pull every pitch.

Through hours of practice in the batting cage, the Yankee coaches slowly helped Jeter retool his swing. They taught him to go with the pitch and to hit it where it was thrown.

As Jeter developed a so-called "inside-out swing," his batting average rose dramatically. The Yankees were pleased that as it did Jeter regained some power, driving the ball with authority to the gaps for extra bases. And when Jeter got on base, he was dangerous. He was beginning to learn how to read pitchers so he could use his speed to steal bases.

He also made progress in the field, although his improvement there took longer. At first he still made a lot of errors — nearly one every other game. Things got so bad that he later admitted, "I was hoping they wouldn't hit another ball to shortstop."

But manager Bill Evers saw plenty of reasons to be optimistic. He noticed that Jeter was making most of his errors for one of two reasons. First, he was inconsistent in the way he approached the ball and threw it. On one play he might charge the ball and throw sidearm on the run. But on a similar play an inning or two later he might stay back and throw overhand. Evers worked with Jeter to play each ball the same way when possible.

Many of the remainder of Jeter's errors stemmed from his poor judgment. On many occasions he'd get to balls that most other shortstops couldn't reach. Although he wouldn't have a chance of throwing the runner out, Jeter often tried to make a spectacular play and would throw the ball away. Other times he'd forget who the batter was, and rush his throw even though the runner was slow.

Jeter knew that he needed help, admitting to a reporter, "I need work on everything — defense, offense, baserunning. I don't feel like I have mastered anything." Evers thought all Jeter's problems were correctable and worked with him to overcome them. By midseason, the frequency of his errors began to drop.

Although a few observers thought Jeter's high number of errors indicated that he might be better suited to play third base, most saw the same potential Evers did. Even though he made 56 errors for the season, *Baseball America* named him the league's Best Defensive Shortstop and Most Exciting Player. With his .295 batting average, 71 RBIs, 18 stolen bases, and 30 extra-base hits, league managers named him the Most Outstanding Prospect. The Yankees were starting to get excited about Jeter.

But they still resisted any temptation to rush him. That winter Jeter played once more in the instructional league, working particularly hard on his defense. Yankee general manager Gene Michael, a former shortstop himself, told Jeter to pay attention to the way star shortstop Cal Ripken of Baltimore fielded the ball, telling him the reason Ripken was so consistent was because "he looks the same way on every play." Michael said later that winter, "[Jeter] started to become more careful. I think he values the baseball more now."

Jeter opened the 1994 season with Tampa, the Yankees' single-A team in the Florida State League. The FSL was considered a much better league than North Carolina's South Atlantic League and promised to provide an accurate gauge of Jeter's progress.

His improvement was dramatic. By midseason his batting average hovered around .330 and he led the league in most offensive categories. While he was still making a few too many errors, he was also getting to balls few other shortstops in baseball could reach.

In late June the Yankees promoted Jeter to Albany in the double-A Eastern League. Most experienced baseball officials consider the jump from single-A to double-A to be the biggest test a young player ever faces. Many prospects fail to make a successful adjustment and their professional baseball careers come to an end.

But Jeter thrived at double-A. If anything, he played even better than he had in single-A. After only a month he was hitting .377.

The Yankees quickly promoted him to their triple-A team in Columbus, Ohio, only one step below the major leagues, and Yankees fans suddenly began paying close attention to his progress. The 1994 Yankees were leading the American League East and looking forward to their first postseason appearance in more than a decade. Their one weakness was the shortstop position, which was shared by veterans Mike Gallego, a fine fielder but a weak hitter, and Randy Velarde, a good hitter but only an average fielder. Some Yankees fans wanted New York to make Jeter their starting shortstop immediately.

But the Yankees remained patient. The major league players and owners were arguing over their next contract and many people expected the players to go on strike before the end of the season. The Yankees knew that if they brought up Jeter and the players went on strike, he would not be allowed to play until the strike was settled. They didn't want to take a chance that his progress would be halted.

In Columbus, Jeter picked up right where he had left off in Albany. He feasted on triple-A pitching and continued to impress everyone in the organization with his improved defensive play and his attitude.

Then it happened. Team owners and major league players could not come to terms and the players went on strike on August 11, bringing the major league season to a halt. Without a major league team to direct, Yankee officials turned their attention toward the minors.

On August 17, Yankee general manager Gene Michael and manager Buck Showalter traveled to Norfolk, Virginia, to watch the Columbus Clippers play the New York Mets' triple-A team. They wanted to see for themselves just how close Jeter was to being ready for the major leagues.

Jeter knew Michael and Showalter were in the ballpark, but he wasn't nervous. Now he was full of confidence.

In his first at bat in the first inning, Norfolk pitcher Juan Castillo left the ball over the plate. Jeter was beginning to recognize the pitches that he could pull, and he turned on the ball, hitting it on a line to left field. It sailed over the fence and caromed off the earthen embankment beyond for a two-run homer to put the Clippers ahead.

Then, in the fourth inning, Jeter proved he knew what he was doing at the plate. The bases were loaded and Norfolk played the infield in, hoping to cut off the run at the plate.

With the bases loaded many young players swing for home runs. More often than not, they end up striking out or popping up.

But Jeter was learning to hit according to the situation. With the infield in, he knew that if he just hit the ball hard, it would probably get through the infield before anyone had time to react.

Sure enough, he got a pitch he could handle and

went with it, driving the ball hard on the ground be-tween the first and second basemen, driving in two runs. Jeter finished the day 2-for-4 with four RBIs in the Clippers' 6–2 win.

Michael and Showalter were impressed, as was Columbus manager Stump Merrill. After the game he said of Jeter, "He's legit [a legitimate prospect]. He's got a chance to be something special."

Norfolk manager Bobby Valentine concurred. "He sticks out in a crowd," he said.

With major league baseball still on strike, causing the World Series to be canceled, Jeter's perfor-mance got the attention of almost everyone, even Yankees fans in New York. Desperate for baseball, several Clipper games were broadcast in New York. Fans liked what they saw.

For the rest of the season, Jeter stood out from the crowd wherever the Clippers played. He fin-ished the season with a flourish, collecting a hit in 11 of his last 19 at bats to end the season with a .349 average in 35 triple-A games. For the season, in three minor league stops Jeter hit a combined .344 with five home runs and 50 stolen bases. His errors dropped by more than half, from 56 in 1993 to only

25 in 1994. Moreover, when Derek was in the lineup his teams compiled a winning percentage of .621. Without him, they barely played .500 baseball.

At the end of the season *Baseball America, The Sporting News, USA Today,* and Topps all named Jeter the minor league player of the year.

Many people expected the Yankees to promote Jeter to the major leagues in 1995. But he was still only twenty years old. In the off-season, while playing in the Arizona Fall League, Jeter started to wear down and got a sore shoulder. The Yankees decided to continue to be patient with him and signed veteran free agent Tony Fernandez to a two-year contract to play shortstop.

To reassure Jeter, Gene Michael called him and told him that he was still very much in New York's plans. In truth, Jeter's meteoric rise in 1994 had taken the Yankees by surprise. He'd played so well they didn't quite believe it. They wanted to make sure his performance hadn't been a fluke.

Jeter began working out with Columbus from the very beginning of training camp. The major leaguers were still on strike. They didn't sign a new contract until April and the season started three weeks late.

Jeter quickly made believers out of those who doubted his 1994 performance. He got off to a fast start at Columbus. After 46 games he was second in the International League in hitting at .354 and fielding more consistently than ever. Then in late May, Yankee shortstop Tony Fernandez injured his rib cage.

Normally, backup infielder Randy Velarde would have filled in at shortstop. But second baseman Pat Kelly was also out with an injury and Velarde was needed to fill in at second base. The Yankees were off to a slow start. If they hoped to qualify for the playoffs they couldn't afford to fall too far behind. They needed some help.

On May 28, the phone rang at the Jeter house in Kalamazoo. Sharlee, then fifteen, answered the phone. On the other end she heard her brother talking excitedly. He asked her to give the phone to his father.

Sharlee handed the phone to Charles Jeter. "Dad," Derek said breathlessly, "I'm out of here."

The Yankees had called him to the major leagues. Derek Jeter's dream was about to come true.

Chapter Six:
1995

Dream Come True

Jeter left immediately for Seattle, where the Yankees were playing the Mariners. Meanwhile, his parents had a decision to make.

As much as they wanted to see their son play his first major league game, Sharlee Jeter had an important tournament game for Kalamazoo Central's softball team. They eventually decided that Charles would fly to Seattle and Dorothy would stay behind to attend Sharlee's softball game.

When Derek arrived in Seattle on May 29, he checked into the team hotel and went straight to the ballpark. When he arrived, he discovered his name on a uniform hanging in a locker.

But it was the number on his uniform that electrified him the most. The New York Yankees, the most storied franchise in baseball, have retired more numbers to honor great players than any other team. In fact, every single-digit number except for 2 and 6 has been retired. Single-digit numbers are only given to players the Yankees expect to be great.

The Yankees gave Derek number 2, sending him a message that they expected him to be an all-time great. That was a lot of pressure for a twenty-year-old. He was thrilled, admitting much later, "When I was a kid, I was always hoping there'd be a jersey left for me with a single digit."

Manager Showalter hadn't called Jeter up just to have him sit on the bench. He told the press, "He will play." When Jeter looked at the lineup card he saw that he was scheduled to start the game at shortstop and hit ninth.

When he took the field for the first time, he could hardly believe it. At first base was the great Don Mattingly. And next to Jeter, playing third base, was perennial batting champion Wade Boggs. Jeter was the youngest active player in the American League and the second-youngest player ever to play for the Yankees.

Jeter was nervous, but he tried not to let it show. He fielded flawlessly, but failed to get a hit in the Yankees' 8–7 loss.

After the game he met with his father to celebrate.

But because the game went into extra innings most downtown Seattle restaurants were closed. The Jeters finally found an open McDonald's and celebrated Derek's first major league game over hamburgers!

The next day Jeter felt much more relaxed. After striking out in his first at bat against the Mariners' Tim Belcher, he singled his next two times up and scored each time in New York's 7–2 loss.

The Yankees were impressed, but cautioned everyone not to expect too much from the young star-to-be. "We're not going to hang the weight of the Yankee world on his shoulders," said Showalter. "We're just going to let him play and support him any way we can."

The Yankees then returned to New York to play California. Jeter was extra excited. He couldn't wait to put on the famous Yankee pinstriped home uniform and take the field at Yankee Stadium, the same place where Babe Ruth, Mickey Mantle, and his own boyhood hero, Dave Winfield, had once played.

His entire family, including his grandmother and other relatives from New Jersey, turned out for his first home game on Friday, June 2. Although Jeter failed to get a hit, he again played his position flawlessly. The next day, with most of the family again in attendance, Jeter singled and walked, and then demonstrated his poise when he told the press, "They [his family] had better seats than we used to get at the Stadium, but I had the better view."

As the season progressed, Jeter continued to play impressively, showing steadiness in the field and getting the occasional timely hit. He shared an apartment with rookie pitcher Mariano Rivera, with whom he'd played in the minor leagues. The fans discovered him, and he quickly became a favorite.

Female fans became particularly enamored of Jeter. His boyish good looks, handsome green eyes, and unmarried status made him an instant favorite of many young female fans. Every day, more and more fan mail for Jeter poured into Yankee Stadium. Every time he took the field, young women squealed his name as if he were a rock star.

But Jeter kept a level head. He told everyone he was just trying to play the game as well as he could. He impressed both the fans and his teammates with his talents and attitude.

But only two weeks after Jeter was called up to the major leagues, Tony Fernandez was healthy again.

Although Jeter had hit .234, fielded well, and ran the bases impressively in his short stint in the majors, Fernandez was still New York's starting shortstop. On June 11, 1995, Showalter told Jeter the club was returning him to Columbus.

Jeter understood the decision, telling the press, "I'm surprised they didn't send me down sooner." Although the club could have kept Jeter on the active roster, he wouldn't have played very much, and they knew that wouldn't help his development.

Privately, the Yankees were thrilled with Jeter, not only for his performance on the field, but also for his poise and professionalism. Some members of the organization began to think that despite the presence of Fernandez, Jeter might be ready to play regularly in 1996.

Although Jeter suffered a brief letdown after returning to Columbus, going into a short slump, he soon started hitting again and continued to play good defense. Jeter was selected for the International League All-Star team and again was among the league leaders in many offensive categories.

Meanwhile the Yankees finally started playing better and were in contention to make the playoffs.

When they slumped in late August, some sportswriters lobbied for a return of Jeter to give the club a spark, but the Yankees still refused to rush him.

Jeter wasn't recalled until after September 1, when major league rosters increase from twenty-five to forty players. But Showalter made it clear that he had no plans to make any lineup changes, saying, "This is no time to be experimenting." As the Yankees secured their wild-card spot in the playoffs, Jeter sat on the bench and learned by watching. He played only two more games.

The Yankees finished second in the A.L. East to the Boston Red Sox, but won the wild-card spot in the playoffs, earning the right to play the A.L. West champion Seattle Mariners. But Jeter was left off the playoff roster.

After taking a two-games-to-none lead over the Mariners, New York dropped the next three games and lost the series. Yankee owner George Steinbrenner, notorious for being one of the most demanding owners in professional sports, was bitterly disappointed by the loss. Losing simply wasn't acceptable, and he wanted to make some changes. As Jeter would soon learn, those changes would involve him.

Chapter Seven:
1996

A Season in the Sun

After visiting his parents in Kalamazoo when the season ended, Jeter went to Tampa to spend the winter. He was determined to make himself the best player he could be. He'd told the press when he'd been sent down to Columbus, "It was good to get a taste of the big leagues. I'll be back." Now that Jeter had achieved his dream, he just wanted to keep dreaming.

While Jeter was working out in Tampa, George Steinbrenner got busy. Despite the fact that Buck Showalter was one of the most respected managers in baseball, Steinbrenner blamed him for the Yankees' loss and forced him out. In November he hired former player and experienced big league manager Joe Torre to replace him.

The press howled, referring to Torre as "Clueless

Joe," for although he'd been a very good player and had managed the Braves, Mets, and Cardinals, he'd never won a World Series. He was widely perceived to be only a temporary solution while Steinbrenner cleaned house.

First baseman Don Mattingly was another off-season casualty. Bothered by a bad back, he wasn't a dangerous hitter anymore. When the Yankees signed free agent first baseman Tino Martinez, Mattingly decided to retire.

New York entered spring training both in transition and under intense pressure to win. Jeter soon got a taste of what it was like to be in the middle of a New York Yankee controversy.

Before spring training started the Yankees decided to give Jeter the opportunity to be the starting shortstop. If he failed, they still had Tony Fernandez.

Initially, Joe Torre was less than enthusiastic about trying the change. He knew that George Steinbrenner wouldn't be satisfied with anything less than a world championship and he knew that would be hard to win with a rookie at shortstop. "I don't know what to expect from Derek," he told the press. "They tell me he's ready."

When training camp opened and Jeter started working out with the starting team, Tony Fernandez got upset. The Yankees considered him an insurance policy in case Jeter failed, but in the meantime they wanted him to play second base. But Fernandez was proud of his abilities and had signed with the Yankees as a shortstop. He demanded a trade.

The situation wasn't helped when Jeter got off to a bit of a rough start in the spring, making several errors. But then he settled down. Every day he played a little better, particularly on defense. He knew that as a shortstop, defense was the most important part of his game. Joe Torre told reporters, "If he hits .250 and plays good defense, we'll be happy."

Late in spring training Tony Fernandez broke his elbow. Now the Yankees had no alternative to playing Jeter.

With only a week left in spring training, Jeter looked like a lock to start the season as the Yankees' number-one shortstop. Then George Steinbrenner got involved.

Steinbrenner had all sorts of advisers working for him. He went to Torre and said, "Some of my advisers tell me they don't think Jeter is ready to play." He wanted to make a trade for a veteran shortstop.

But by now Jeter had won Torre over. Torre had seen him improve day by day and he absolutely loved his attitude. Just as Don Mattingly had taught him, Jeter practiced as if he never knew who was watching. And unlike many rookies, who tried to hide their lack of confidence under a veneer of cockiness, Jeter seemed to understand from the very beginning just how a rookie was supposed to behave. He accepted his teammates ribbing good-naturedly and acted respectful toward everyone, even referring to his manager as "Mr. Torre," a practice he continues to this day. Even the Yankee veterans were impressed.

Torre told Steinbrenner he thought it was too late to make a change, and told the press. "It's obvious that keeping him in the minors will no longer do him any good." Steinbrenner reluctantly agreed, but he made it clear to Torre that if Jeter failed, he would hold the manager responsible.

Jeter finished spring training with an impressive .288 batting average. On the precipice of the season, he was both excited and confident. "This is something I've been waiting for my whole life," he said. "I love New York, I like the fans, I like the stadium." Even George Steinbrenner was starting to come around, telling the press, "We'll be patient with him. Every year you look for Derek Jeter to stumble, and he doesn't. . . . I'm telling you, he could be one of the special ones."

Jeter was one of the most ballyhooed rookies in Yankee history. Not since Mickey Mantle had arrived on the scene in 1952 had so much been expected of one player.

The Yankees started the 1996 season in Cleveland on April 2. Jeter was spectacular from the very beginning.

As the Yankees waited to take the field, Jeter approached Joe Torre, a look of concern on his face. The manager expected the rookie to ask for some advice or words of encouragement.

Instead, Jeter looked Torre in the eye and asked, "You okay?" He thought his manager looked nervous and wanted to make sure he was all right! Jeter wasn't nervous at all!

He soon proved it. In the second inning Cleveland catcher Sandy Alomar hit a hard ground ball to

Jeter's right, deep into what is referred to as the "hole."

The ability to make the play in the hole is what separates great shortstops from good ones, for the play tests every skill a shortstop must have, from his speed and quickness to his footwork and his arm.

As soon as the ball was hit, Jeter broke to his right and raced after the ball. He backhanded the ball cleanly, transferred it to his throwing hand, then as his momentum carried him toward left field, he jumped in the air and threw a perfect strike to Tino Martinez.

"Out!" The umpire shot his hand into the air as the throw beat Alomar. Yankee fans all around the country watching on television turned to each other and smiled. The kid could play!

Then in the fifth inning with the Yankees leading 1–0 against veteran pitcher Dennis Martinez, Jeter led off. He got a pitch he could handle and turned on the ball, swinging hard.

Crack! The ball sailed over the left field fence for a home run to give the Yankees a 2–0 lead! It was Derek Jeter's first big league home run. He tried to suppress a smile as he ran around the bases, but as soon as he reached the dugout he broke into a wide grin.

But Jeter wasn't done yet. In the seventh inning Cleveland shortstop Omar Vizquel lofted a fly ball to shallow center field. Yankee outfielder Bernie Williams started racing in as Jeter sprinted out.

Jeter knew that a shortstop is supposed to go after outfield pop-ups until he hears the outfielder call him off. He looked over his shoulder as he tracked the ball and waited to hear from Williams.

"You, you, you!" he heard the center fielder shout. The ball wasn't hit deep enough for Williams to reach.

Looking almost directly over his head, Jeter ran and ran and ran. As the ball descended, he reached out at the last possible second with his glove.

He caught it! Out! The spectacular catch even brought Cleveland fans to their feet, and preserved Yankee pitcher David Cone's 2–0 lead in the eventual 7–1 New York win. After the game, Cone stated the obvious, saying, "That was a major league play." Joe Torre said simply, "He did everything today."

Then the next day all Jeter did in the second game of the season was go 3 for 3.

Keyed by Jeter, the Yankees jumped out to a quick start to the season. They had expected him to play well, and thought that he would be good, but Jeter was playing great. He got even more attention on May 15 when he caught the final out of teammate Dwight Gooden's no-hitter.

Jeter was one of several young shortstops making a big impact in the majors. Across town, the Mets' Rey Ordonez was already being compared to the best fielding shortstops in the history of baseball, such as Ozzie Smith. The Mariners' Alex Rodriguez, although technically not a rookie, was a year younger than Jeter and hitting with as much power as any shortstop in baseball.

Jeter and Rodriguez were close. When Derek was in his second year of pro baseball, Rodriguez had been named High School Player of the Year, just as Jeter had. He'd felt overwhelmed by all the attention and had called Jeter for advice. The two young players discovered they had a lot in common and became good friends. They still call each other a couple of times a week, and when the Yankees visit

Seattle, or vice versa, they even stay in each other's apartment.

Together, they represented a new breed of major league shortstops. In the past, most shortstops had been small, speedy, good fielding players from whom little offense was expected. They hadn't been expected to hit for a high average or for much power. The few that did, like Chicago's Ernie Banks in the 1960s and Baltimore star Cal Ripken, were considered unique.

But neither Banks nor Ripken had the combination of size, speed, and strength of Jeter and Rodriguez. They were revolutionizing the position with their play.

The Yankees pulled out to a big lead in the American League East, then slumped when pitcher David Cone went down with an aneurysm in his right (pitching) shoulder. Baltimore nearly caught up with the Yankees, but Cone, remarkably, returned to the lineup and the Yankees were able to hold the Orioles off, winning the division with a 92–70 record.

The Yankees had lots of stars. Pitcher Andy Pettitte won 21 games and John Wetteland saved 43, while both Tino Martinez and Bernie Williams knocked in over 100 runs and hit more than 20 home runs. But in many people's minds the player who made the biggest impact on the 1996 Yankees was Derek Jeter. The rookie whom Joe Torre hoped would hit .250 hit .314 for the season. In the second half of the season he hit over .350! Moreover, he displayed more power than he ever had in the minor leagues, cracking ten home runs with 78 RBIs despite hitting ninth for most of the season. And his defense was nothing short of spectacular. He made the routine plays look effortless and the spectacular plays look routine. The few errors he made usually came when he made a bad decision, trying to make an impossible play.

Jeter and his teammates looked forward to the postseason. The young shortstop knew that on the Yankees, the regular season really didn't matter. To owner George Steinbrenner and the Yankees' fans, nothing less than a world championship would ever be satisfactory.

Some observers didn't give the Yankees much of a chance in the postseason. Incredibly, one of the rea-

sons was the presence of Derek Jeter. Rookie shortstops were supposed to crumble under the pressure
of postseason play. Only a few teams in baseball history had ever won a World Series with a rookie at
shortstop.

But Joe Torre disagreed. He'd seen enough of his
young shortstop to sense that he was different, telling reporters, "Big games and big situations don't
scare him."

In the first round of the playoffs the Yankees
played the powerful Texas Rangers. At first, it appeared as if Jeter's critics had been right. In the series opener, a 6–2 New York loss, Jeter had left six
runners on base, including the bases loaded in the
sixth inning.

The next game was huge. In a best-of-five series,
it's almost impossible to come back after losing the
first two games. Jeter was determined not to let his
subpar play in game one affect him.

Game two was a close contest, one in which the
game hung in the balance on every pitch and every
play. After falling behind, 4–1, the Yankees clawed
back to tie the game and take it into extra innings.

With the score still tied, 4–4, Jeter led off the twelfth inning with a single. Then he moved to second on a walk.

As Jeter took his lead off second base, he watched Yankee third base coach Willie Randolph closely. Randolph flashed New York third baseman Charlie Hayes the bunt sign.

As the pitcher wound up, Jeter danced off second. He wanted to get a good jump and make sure he made third base, but he also had to be careful. If he strayed too far off the base and Hayes missed the bunt, Texas catcher Ivan Rodriguez could throw him out.

Hayes squared around and dropped the ball toward third base. Jeter took off.

Texas third baseman Dean Palmer fielded the ball, but rushed his throw to first. It bounced wide of the bag.

Jeter had been watching the play and saw the ball go wide. Without breaking stride he rounded third and raced home, scoring easily to give the Yanks a 5–4 win.

Afterward, he lectured the press, saying, "If I don't get a hit, you guys say I'm pressing. If I do, you say I'm not. I feel the same way tonight as I did yesterday."

Jeter continued his special play in game three. After Jeter and second baseman Mariano Duncan got their signals crossed and left second base uncovered in the fifth inning, which eventually allowed Texas to take a 2–1 lead, Jeter had a shot at redemption when he led off the ninth inning. With the game on the line he was determined to make up for his mistake. New York was only three outs away from defeat.

But Derek singled, and then scored on Tim Raines's single, and the Yankees went on to win, 3–2. Jeter had come through once again!

New York then defeated Texas, 6–4, in the final game to win the series and the right to play Baltimore in the League Championship Series for the American League pennant. All Derek had done in the series was hit .412, second on the team to Bernie Williams's .438.

So far, Derek's rookie season had been the stuff dreams are made of. But neither Jeter nor Yankees fans were ready to wake up.

Chapter Eight:
1996

Attaboy, Champ!

The American League Championship Series versus Baltimore opened in New York. Many people expected the Orioles to beat the Yankees. They had looked great in defeating Cleveland. In the regular season they had hit a major league–record 257 home runs and were led by stars such as Cal Ripken, Rafael Palmeiro, Roberto Alomar, and Brady Anderson.

The opening game of the series was another close, hard-fought contest. The Yankees jumped ahead, 1–0, in the first inning, but Baltimore tied the contest in the second. New York went ahead again, 2–1, in the bottom of the inning, but Baltimore scored two runs to make it 3–2 in the third inning. Each team added another run, and entering the eighth inning, the Orioles still led, 4–3. They turned the game over to their bullpen needing only six more outs to win the game.

Jeter came up in the eighth inning with one out and no one on base. In such a high-pressure situation, many managers would have pinch-hit for a rookie with someone more experienced. But that thought never crossed manager Joe Torre's mind. Jeter had proven himself time and time again.

Yankees fans applauded loudly when Jeter stepped to the plate. He was one of the few Yankee players who didn't seem to be struggling He had already collected an infield hit on what looked to be a routine ground ball to Oriole shortstop Cal Ripken by running hard all the way to first base and beating Ripken's throw. So far, the rookie had outplayed the legend.

On the mound for the Orioles was right-handed reliever Armando Benitez. Although he didn't always know where he was throwing the ball, Benitez threw hard. His fastball regularly reached speeds of up to ninety-eight miles per hour.

When Jeter stepped in, he told himself to go with the pitch and not try to pull it. That was particularly important against a hard thrower like Benitez. Jeter knew that if he tried to pull the ball, he'd probably get jammed and either pop up or hit a weak ground ball.

The Yankees needed base runners. With the top of the order coming up, all Jeter wanted to do was get on base. He just wanted to hit the ball the opposite way.

Meanwhile, in section 31 in the box seats just beyond the right field fence, a twelve-year-old boy from New Jersey named Jeffrey Maier moved down from his seat to the aisle in front of the stands atop the ten-foot-high right field fence. Maier was a huge Yankees fan who played center field on his Little League team. Like Derek Jeter many years before, he had brought his glove to the game hoping that he'd have an opportunity to catch a home run.

Benitez wound up and threw the ball to Jeter. The pitch was a blur.

But Jeter did what he planned to do. Instead of pulling the ball, he went the other way, and got the fat part of the bat on the ball.

Crack! He hit a slicing fly ball to right field.

Oriole right fielder Tony Tarasco tracked the ball and drifted back toward the fence. Jeter hadn't hit the ball especially well, but the fence in right field in Yankee Stadium isn't very deep, particularly toward the line.

Jeter tossed his bat down and started running toward first base. He saw Tarasco drifting back and hoped the ball would reach the wall.

Tarasco had the ball in his sights. He felt the warning track under his feet as he drifted back and knew the fence was only a few yards away. But he saw the ball dropping fast, and knew Jeter hadn't hit it quite far enough for a home run. He felt for the wall with his right hand and reached up with his left hand to catch the ball.

Rounding first base, Derek Jeter saw Tarasco reach up to catch the ball. Umpire Richie Garcia raced down the right field line to get in position to make the call if Tarasco caught the ball.

In the stands, Jeffrey Maier couldn't believe it. The ball was coming right at him! Almost without thinking, he got ready to catch it. As he did, several other fans who had the same idea jostled him.

Jeffrey closed his eyes and stuck his glove out over the wall to catch the ball. Directly below him, Tony Tarasco opened his glove to make the catch.

Thwack! The ball struck Maier's glove. Tarasco closed his glove — and caught only air.

The ball bounced up off Maier's glove, over the fence, and into the stands. Derek Jeter kept running. He'd seen Tarasco try for the catch, but saw that he didn't have the ball. Now the right fielder stood at the wall and pointed up.

Umpire Richie Garcia didn't hesitate. He waved his hand in a circle, signaling a home run. Yankee Stadium exploded in cheers. Jeffrey Maier scrambled for the loose baseball. He didn't get it.

Orioles' manager Davey Johnson jumped out of the dugout and ran toward Garcia, as did Tarasco. They argued that Maier had reached into the field of play and interfered with the ball, knocking it over the fence. Without his "help," they argued, Tarasco would have caught the ball. They wanted Garcia to rule interference and call Jeter out.

Television replays clearly showed that Johnson and Tarasco were correct. But baseball doesn't use replays to make calls. Garcia's decision stood. Johnson got thrown out of the ball game.

The game was tied, 4–4! A home run for Derek Jeter!

The Yankees were able to hold off the Orioles, and the game entered extra innings. In the eleventh, Bernie Williams hit a walk-off home run to left field to end the game and give New York a 5–4 win and 1–0 lead in the series.

But after the game, all anybody wanted to talk about was Jeffrey Maier and Jeter's home run. The press had tracked Maier down. To New York fans, he was a hero. Baltimore fans thought he was a cheat.

The Orioles were disconsolate and blamed the play for their loss, ignoring the fact that they had made a number of mistakes throughout the game. "It was like a magic trick," said Tarasco of the play. "I was ready to close my glove, and the ball just disappeared out of midair."

But Derek Jeter wasn't complaining. He was powerless to do anything about the call, anyway. Although the umpire clearly had made the wrong call, he knew that over the course of a season umpires miss many calls. Some go against you and some go for you. In the long run, they even out. Besides, he knew that had the Orioles benefited from a similar call, they wouldn't have complained. Such plays are a part of baseball.

In an interview after the game, Maier was both happy and a little bewildered. "I don't know why they should be mad at me," he said of the Orioles. "I'm just a twelve-and-a-half-year-old kid trying to get a ball." The next day, Jeffrey's father called Tarasco and had Jeffrey apologize. Tarasco was understanding and told him, "I would have done exactly the same thing."

Derek Jeter had a similar response. When reporters asked him after the game if there was anything he'd like to say to Jeffrey Maier, Jeter looked up and with a wry smile said, laughing, "Attaboy."

The Orioles came back to win game two, 5–2, to tie up the series. Then, in game three, with the Yanks trailing, 2–1, in the eighth, Jeter started a comeback with a leadoff double. New York stormed from behind to win, 5–2. The Yankees then surged to win the next two games and take the series four games to one. Jeter was nothing short of spectacular, leading the team with ten hits, batting .417, stealing two bases, and outplaying Cal Ripken at shortstop. In fact, Jeter recorded the last out of game five when he went deep into the hole to field a hot smash from Ripken's bat, then threw the star out from his knees to end the series in spectacular fashion. Although Bernie Williams, who hit .474 with two home runs, was named League Championship Series MVP, Derek Jeter had been just as valuable.

"Sometimes he surprises me with the things he does," said Torre afterward.

Torre and the Yankees were hoping Jeter had a few more surprises up his sleeve, because the Yankees were on their way to the World Series against the powerful Atlanta Braves. Paced by their tremendous pitching staff featuring Greg Maddux, Tom Glavine, and John Smoltz, the Braves were defending world champs. Most observers expected them to beat the Yankees easily.

At first it appeared as if they would. In the first two games of the Series, played in New York, the Braves thumped the Yankees, 12–1, then shut them out, 4–0. When the two clubs arrived in Atlanta for game three, no one was giving the Yankees a chance to win. One Atlanta newspaper ran a headline that asked, "Why Bother To Play It Out?" and a sportswriter wrote that not even the 1927 Yankees, considered by many the best team in history, could beat the Braves.

At the beginning of game three, the Yankees knew they had to score to put some pressure on Atlanta. Tim Raines walked to start the game, then Jeter, hitting second in the batting order, made a perfect sacrifice bunt to send Raines to second. Bernie Williams knocked him in, and New York led, 1–0.

With a lead, Yankee pitcher David Cone was tough and New York went on to win, 5–2. But in game four they fell behind, 6–0.

Once again, Derek Jeter keyed the comeback, starting a three-run rally with a leadoff single. The Yankees tied the fourth game, 6–6, in the eighth, and the game went into extra innings when neither team could score in the ninth. Then, in the tenth, Raines walked again and Jeter singled. That was the start the Yankees needed. They went on to score twice to tie the Series at two games apiece. When Andy Pettitte hurled a shutout in game five, the Yankees suddenly had the Braves on the ropes.

The Series returned to New York for game six. With the game scoreless in the third inning, Paul O'Neill doubled and Joe Girardi tripled to center field off Braves ace Greg Maddux to make the score 1–0. Jeter then came up and singled Girardi home before stealing second and scoring himself on Wade Boggs's single. The Yankees had a 3–0 lead.

The Braves battled back with a single run in the fourth, but Jeter snuffed the rally by turning a nifty double play. Though the Braves added one more run, when third baseman Charlie Hayes caught a pop-up for the final out, the Yankees were world champions.

Jeter ran and jumped into the big pileup of players on the pitcher's mound, then joined his teammates in the dugout for a celebration. No Yankee in the postseason had been more consistent or played a better all-around game. Jeter had made precious few mistakes — only a couple of meaningless errors — and had come through in the clutch virtually every time the Yankees needed him, hitting a combined .361 in the postseason.

A few days later, New York honored the team with a ticker tape parade and a celebration at City Hall.

"This year has been a fantasy," Jeter said. "A dream come true. It's been an absolutely perfect year."

For Derek Jeter, it was just the beginning.

Chapter Nine:
1997

Sophomore Slump?

The baseball phrase "sophomore slump" refers to the letdown many players experience in their second season in the major leagues. After having some success in their rookie season, many young players take it easy in their second year. They think they've got the game of baseball all figured out and they don't have to work as hard to stay in the big leagues as they did to get there. As a result, many players falter in their second, or sophomore, season.

No one had to warn Jeter about the sophomore slump. He'd heard all about it and was determined not to let it happen to him. When a reporter asked him if he was worried about it, Jeter said, "Everyone's talking about it — it makes me work that much harder."

Soon after the World Series he traveled to Tampa

and rented an apartment. Jeter, several other younger Yankees, and his friend Alex Rodriguez all worked out together to prepare for the upcoming season.

But Jeter didn't spend the entire off-season in Tampa. In the wake of the Series, he had become a big celebrity. He appeared on a host of television programs, including *The Late Show with David Letterman* and *Seinfeld.* And as one of the few Yankees who lived in Manhattan, he was often asked to attend charity functions in New York and lend his name to good causes.

He knew there was no way he would be able to accommodate every such request. But he still wanted to help people out, to somehow share his good fortune with those less fortunate.

From the very beginning of his career Jeter realized that kids look up to athletes as role models, and he tried to live up to that image. His own parents did a great job steering him clear of trouble, so he decided to try to do the same for the kids that look up to him as a hero.

With the assistance of his father and his agent, Casey Close, Jeter created the Turn 2 Foundation, so named because the phrase "turn two" is baseball slang for a double play. The goal of the foundation is to support programs to prevent and treat teenage abuse of drugs and alcohol and to provide alternative activities and scholarships both in the Kalamazoo area and in metropolitan New York. Jeter donates to the foundation himself and solicits contributions from sponsors and corporations, as well. In fact, Jeter only agrees to do endorsements for companies that agree in turn to support his foundation.

"I believe it's important to give something back to the community," Jeter said when he created the foundation. "I want to show kids there's another way to go." Although the charity started out very small, over the years it has grown. Dr. Charles Jeter, with his background as a substance abuse counselor, now manages the foundation full-time. "It involves a different relationship for us," said Dr. Jeter when asked what it's like to work with his son. "It brings us closer together."

In November, Jeter's fame only increased. To no one's surprise, he was the unanimous choice as American League Rookie of the Year, only the fifth unanimous pick since the award was created. True to form, Jeter downplayed his individual achievements. "Winning a world championship is best," he said, "even [better] than winning this award." But success, Jeter learned, came with a certain price.

As a big celebrity, Jeter was now recognized everywhere he went. Whenever he was out in public, people clamored for his autograph. Even when he was driving his car, someone would spot him and all of a sudden Jeter would realize he was being followed. Young women he didn't know would stake out his apartment or approach him in public. Although he enjoyed the attention, at the same time it could be a little bit frightening.

In New York, the media capital of the world, nearly everything Jeter said or did was news. People wanted to know every little detail of his life, such as his favorite food (chicken parmesan), his favorite music (R&B and hip-hop), his middle name (Sanderson), and even his favorite color (blue). He found his activities reported in gossip columns whenever he was in New York.

Many athletes succumb to the pressure of a public life and end up either losing focus or partying too much, but Jeter had managed to keep a level head, a fact not lost on his friends and teammates. Fellow

Yankee Chili Davis later commented, "You look at him and you've got to tip your hat to his parents. They did a good job raising him. He knows right from wrong. Not too many young players (who) come into this game and have that kind of success that early realize that."

Jeter answered any lingering questions about whether he'd let success go to his head when he arrived in spring training. He'd added ten or fifteen pounds of muscle and was in the best shape of his life. Moreover, he was still open to taking advice from his teammates. Both Yankee coach Willie Randolph and veteran backup infielder Luis Sojo worked with Jeter to improve his fielding, suggesting that he make a few minor changes in his approach.

But after getting off to a quick start at the beginning of the season, Jeter soon learned another reason why so many good young players suffer from a sophomore slump. In his rookie year, Jeter had been something of a surprise to the other teams in the league. Because he usually hit ninth in the batting order, pitchers hadn't worried too much about him. He had seen a lot of fastballs and got a lot of good pitches to hit.

But in 1997, Jeter was no secret. Joe Torre moved him up from ninth in the batting order. Depending upon who was pitching for the other team, Jeter hit either seventh, second, or first in the Yankee batting order. Jeter discovered pitchers were suddenly being a lot more careful with him. He didn't see nearly as many strikes. Most pitchers, knowing he tried to hit to the opposite field, tried to jam him with fastballs inside. Then, when they got ahead in the count, they got him out with breaking balls or off-speed pitches on the corner as they took advantage of his aggressiveness.

When Jeter stayed patient, and laid off balls early in the count, he hit well. But when he started chasing pitches and got behind in the count, he was easy to put out. After the first two months of the season his batting average hovered around .250. People were beginning to whisper that Jeter's performance in 1996 had been a fluke. Meanwhile the Mariners' Alex Rodriguez was having a tremendous season, and Boston Red Sox rookie shortstop Nomar Garciaparra was tearing up the league. A year earlier, some observers had considered Jeter the best shortstop in the American League. Now, he wasn't even on the shortlist.

But in midseason Tim Raines, the Yankees' lead-off hitter, was injured. Joe Torre moved Jeter into the leadoff slot full-time.

As a leadoff hitter, Jeter's primary job was to get on base any way he could. He forced himself to start taking pitches and stopped swinging at pitches off the corner. As soon as he did, he forced pitchers to throw him strikes. All of a sudden he started hitting again, pulling his average back up to around .300, where it remained even after Raines returned to the lineup and Jeter was dropped down to second again.

As a team, the Yankees' performance in 1997 mirrored that of Jeter. After a good start they slumped and fell far behind Baltimore before going on a tear. Although they finished second to the Orioles in the American League East, they still managed to win 96 games and qualify for the playoffs as a wild-card team. They hoped to vindicate their second-place finish in the division with another world championship.

In the first game of the playoffs against Cleveland, the Yankees fell behind before rallying to tie in the sixth inning on Tim Raines's three-run homer. That brought Jeter up to the plate.

Jeter knew what to expect from Cleveland relief pitcher Eric Plunk. The six-foot-six-inch former Yankee threw hard. Jeter expected to see some fastballs.

But on the first two pitches, that's all Derek did. He saw them, but he didn't hit them and fell behind, 0–2.

Now Jeter had to be careful. He didn't want to strike out. He had to be ready for anything.

Plunk wound up and threw. He meant to throw the ball on the corner, but it drifted over the plate.

Pow! Derek exploded and jerked the ball over the left field wall for a home run! The Yankees led, 7–6.

The crowd at Yankee Stadium cheered long and hard. Jeter reluctantly stuck his head out of the dugout and waved his cap in a curtain call.

Paul O'Neill then followed with another home run, the Yanks' third in a row, to put New York ahead, 8–6. But Derek's home run proved to be the difference.

Jeter refused to accept much credit. "I think the fans blew it out," he said, laughing.

The next night, despite another home run by Jeter, the Indians won, 7–5, to tie the series. In game three in Cleveland, New York won, 6–1, with Jeter collecting two hits and two walks.

New York appeared on the precipice of victory in game four as they led, 2–0, with two outs in the eighth inning. Then, only four outs away from advancing to the League Championship Series, the Yankees' normally reliable bullpen fell apart. Cleveland came back to win the game and tie the series.

Cleveland jumped ahead in game five and held on to win, 4–3, to end New York's season. Jeter summed up everyone's feelings when he said simply, "We blew it. We thought we were the better team and then we got beat."

Next year, he promised himself, he wouldn't let that happen.

Chapter Ten:
1998

Unstoppable, Unbeatable, Incredible!

Yankee owner George Steinbrenner simply wasn't satisfied with anything less than a world championship. Determined to reach the World Series again, he made a number of changes in the off-season. Steinbrenner made Brian Cashman his new general manager, traded for Minnesota Twins second baseman Chuck Knoblauch, and signed Cuban refugee pitcher Orlando "El Duque" Hernandez.

Just a week after the season-ending loss, Jeter demonstrated his commitment to the 1998 season by buying a house in Tampa and beginning his workouts. Although Jeter had played spectacularly in the postseason, his regular season numbers were little changed from those of his rookie year. In fact, some observers were saying he had actually slipped. After all, they argued, his batting average had dropped twenty-three points to .291 and he had struck out 125 times.

A few critics offered that Jeter had had too much success too soon. After all, he'd already fulfilled his dreams. What could possibly be left?

But Jeter knew that playing for the Yankees was different from playing on other teams. Given New York's winning tradition, one world championship doesn't mean very much. As a member of the Yankees, he knew that greatness was measured by only one thing — the number of championship rings a player earns. Hall-of-Famer Yogi Berra had played on the most world championship teams — ten. For himself, Jeter had already answered the question, "What do you dream for when your dreams come true?" He had simply created a bigger dream. He wanted to win as many championships as possible.

The 1998 Yankees all shared the same dream. Jeter jumped out of the box in spring training by hitting .381 with seven extra-base hits and leading the Yankees in RBIs. Then, after the team began the season by losing four of their first six games, leading to some wild speculation that manager Joe Torre was about to be fired, the Yankees began playing like

Derek Jeter goes airborne while trying to make a play at first after forcing B. J. Surhoff out at second.

Derek Jeter slams a long ball that was ruled a home run after Yankee fan Jeff Maier caught it in the stands.

High fives between Derek Jeter and pitcher John Wetteland after they beat the Atlanta Braves to take a three games to two lead in the 1996 World Series.

The glove is quicker than the steal—Derek Jeter beats Atlanta Brave Marquis Grissom to the bag during game six of the 1996 World Series.

Derek Jeter is surrounded by celebrating teammates—they've just won the 1998 American League Championship.

Derek Jeter takes time before a game to sign autographs.

AP/Wide World Photos

2000 All-Star Game starting shortstop Derek Jeter is all smiles after hitting a two-run single. He was named the game's MVP, the first time a Yankee was so honored.

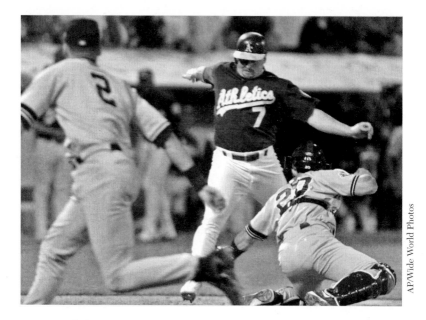

In one of the greatest plays in baseball history, Derek Jeter throws Jeremy Giambi out at home after nabbing a wild throw into the dugout during game three of the 2001 American League Division Series.

Derek Jeter leaps into the arms of his teammates after hitting a game-winning homer in the 10th inning of game four of the 2001 World Series.

In one of his many outstanding plays of the 2002 season, Derek Jeter slides safely into third on a steal.

Derek Jeter's Year-by-Year Batting Stats

Year	Club	Avg.	Games	At Bats	Runs	Hits	2B	3B	HR	RBI
1995	Yankees	.250	15	48	5	12	4	1	0	7
1996	Yankees	.314	157	582	104	183	25	6	10	78
1997	Yankees	.291	159	654	116	190	31	7	10	70
1998	Yankees	.324	149	626	127	203	25	8	19	84
1999	Yankees	.349	158	627	134	219	37	9	24	102
2000	Yankees	.339	148	593	119	201	31	4	15	73
2001	Yankees	.311	150	614	110	191	35	3	21	74
2002	Yankees	.297	157	644	124	191	26	0	18	75
2003	Yankees	.324	119	482	87	156	25	3	10	52
2004	Yankees	.292	154	643	111	188	44	1	23	78
2005	Yankees	.309	159	654	122	202	25	5	19	70
2006	Yankees	.343	154	623	118	214	39	3	14	97
2007	Yankees	.322	156	639	102	206	39	4	12	73
2008	Yankees	.300	150	596	88	179	25	3	11	69
2009	Yankees	.334	153	634	107	212	27	1	18	66
2010*	Yankees	.268	155	653	110	175	30	3	10	66
Career*		.314	2293	9312	1684	2922	468	61	234	1134

Derek Jeter's Year-by-Year Fielding Stats

Year	Club	Pos.	G	GS	E	DP	FLD%
1995	Yankees	SS	15	14	2	7	.962
1996	Yankees	SS	157	156	22	83	.969
1997	Yankees	SS	159	159	18	87	.975
1998	Yankees	SS	148	148	9	82	.986
1999	Yankees	SS	158	158	14	87	.978
2000	Yankees	SS	148	148	24	77	.961
2001	Yankees	SS	150	150	15	68	.974
2002	Yankees	SS	156	156	14	69	.977
2003	Yankees	SS	118	118	14	51	.968
2004	Yankees	SS	154	154	13	96	.981
2005	Yankees	SS	157	157	15	96	.979
2006	Yankees	SS	150	149	15	81	.975
2007	Yankees	SS	155	153	18	104	.970
2008	Yankees	SS	148	147	12	69	.979
2009	Yankees	SS	150	147	8	75	.986
2010*	Yankees	SS	149	148	6	93	.989
Total*			2272	2262	219	1225	.976

*As of September 30, 2010

Derek Jeter's Career Highlights

1995:
Made major league debut on May 29
Named to International League All-Star team

1996:
Voted American League Rookie of the Year
Member of the World Series championship team

1997:
Led American League with 748 plate appearances

1998:
Named to All-Star team
Broke Major League record for most runs scored by a shortstop in his first three full seasons (347)
Named American League Player of the Month for August
Member of the World Series championship team

1999:
Named to All-Star team
Member of the World Series championship team

2000:
Named to All-Star Team
Named All-Star MVP
Named World Series MVP
Member of the World Series championship team

2001:
Named to All-Star Team
Member of the American League championship team

2002:
Named to All-Star Team
Member of the American League championship team
Awarded ESPY: Play of the Year

2003:
Named Captain of New York Yankees
Member of the American League championship team

2004:
Named to All-Star Team
Gold Glove

2005:
Gold Glove

2006:
Named to All-Star Team
Gold Glove
Silver Slugger
AL Hank Aaron Award

2007:
Named to All-Star Team
Silver Slugger

2008:
Named to All-Star Team
Silver Slugger

2009:
Named to All-Star Team
Silver Slugger
Gold Glove
Captain of World Series championship team
Hank Aaron Award
Roberto Clemente Award
Sports Illustrated Sportsman of the Year

they were afraid to lose another game. They almost succeeded.

Jeter got off to a particularly good start, and on May 17, pitcher David Wells hurled a perfect game, lifting New York's record to 28–9. Already, people were beginning to say the Yankees had the division title all wrapped up. By the end of May, Jeter was hitting almost .350 and was among the league leaders in most offensive categories. Joe Torre called him "the MVP on this club to this point."

New York's great performance on the field led the press to look off the field for some excitement. Once again, Jeter gave them something to write about.

Jeter had started dating pop singer Mariah Carey. In addition to being young and famous, they had quite a bit in common. Each was biracial. Like Jeter, Carey had a black father and a white mother.

For the first couple months of the season, the press just couldn't get enough of the budding romance. One day they would report that the two were getting married. The next day they'd report that the romance was off.

Fans picked up on it, and when the Yankees played on the road some would taunt Jeter with chants of "Ma-ri-ah, Ma-ri-ah!" In Chicago, they even played Mariah Carey songs over the loud-speaker every time Jeter came to bat. Some of Jeter's younger female fans were crushed.

He took the attention in stride, although he some-times complained that the press was making things up. But the romance eventually cooled and in early June, Jeter and Carey announced they were just friends.

Actually, Jeter has a hard time finding a steady girlfriend. He's cautious and wants to make sure that anyone he dates is interested in him as a person and not just attracted to his fame. Jeter once joked to a reporter that any girl he goes out with "has to get by my mom and my sister. It takes a lot to pass that test."

Everything was going smoothly for Jeter, on and off the field. Then, in late June, he received a scare. While checking his swing he pulled a muscle in his abdomen. For the first time in his career he had to go on the disabled list and was out of the lineup for over two weeks.

When Jeter returned it took him several weeks to get back on track. At the All-Star break New York's record was a spectacular 67–20. Alex Rodriguez was deservedly voted to the starting lineup for the A.L. All-Stars, but Jeter made the team for the first time, as a reserve.

Everyone in baseball was beginning to realize just how good Jeter had become. He'd matured in every area of the game. In the field, he was almost on par with the Indians' Omar Vizquel, widely considered the best fielding shortstop in the game. He had also become a complete hitter, hitting for power and average. And he was almost unstoppable on the bases. He was one of the most improved players in baseball, and he'd been pretty good to start with!

He had also become a team leader. When pitcher David Wells expressed his displeasure at an error made by another Yankee during a game, it was Derek Jeter who approached him and said, "We don't show you up when you make a bad pitch." Wells apologized.

Interestingly enough, Jeter was one of only two or three Yankees to be having a career year. Most of the Yankees were simply playing well and no one on the team was having an off year. The Yankees just kept winning and winning at a record pace.

Yet as they did, hardly anybody noticed. Most baseball fans were focused on the home run race between Mark McGwire and Sammy Sosa, each of whom would eventually break Roger Maris's single-season record of 61.

That was fine with the Yankees. They just wanted to keep winning, and they did, clinching a playoff berth on August 29, the earliest date ever. They won their 100th game of the season on September 4 and snagged the division title on September 9. That game, Jeter cracked two home runs — his 18th and 19th for the season, a Yankee record for a shortstop — over Yankee Stadium's distant center field wall. The Yankees rolled to 114 regular-season wins, the second highest total in history. Only the 1906 Chicago White Sox had won more regular-season games — 116.

Jeter finished the year with a .324 average, third in the league to teammate Bernie Williams's league-leading .339. He made only nine errors and later finished third in voting for league MVP.

But Jeter and his teammates knew that despite their enormous number of wins, unless they won the World Series they'd be remembered as losers.

The 1954 Cleveland Indians won 111 games, but all they were remembered for was losing the World Series in four straight games to the New York Giants. And as good as the Yankees had been playing, winning the World Series was hardly certain. As if to remind them of this, the team received a bad omen just as the playoffs were getting under way. The team learned that designated hitter Darryl Strawberry, who'd cracked 24 home runs, had colon cancer and wouldn't be able to play.

But the team rallied. In the first round of the playoffs the Yankees faced the potent Texas Rangers. For the second time in three years, New York's starting pitchers dominated the Rangers. David Wells, Andy Pettitte, and David Cone all pitched great.

Good thing, because neither Jeter nor his teammates hit very well. Nevertheless, the Yankees scored just enough runs to beat Texas in three straight games, 2–0, 3–1, and 4–0. Although Jeter collected only a single hit, he may have made the play of the series in game one when he snuffed out a Texas rally by fielding Ranger Rusty Greer's slow ground ball and nipping him at first.

The Yanks met Cleveland in the LCS, looking for

revenge. They hadn't forgotten that Cleveland had knocked them out of the playoffs in 1997.

New York's bats came alive in the opener. Chuck Knoblauch singled to start the game, and then Jeter singled, as did Paul O'Neill and Bernie Williams. The Yanks were off to a good start.

In the fourth inning, Jeter made a play that had the fans buzzing. Cleveland third baseman Travis Fryman spanked a ground ball deep into the hole between short and third for an apparent single.

Jeter, playing deep, ran to his right, off the skinned part of the infield into shallow left field. In a full sprint he backhanded the ball, and as his momentum carried him farther into shallow left field, he jumped in the air, somehow turned, and threw across his body. First baseman Tino Martinez stretched out and the throw just beat Fryman.

Staked to an early lead and backed by such spectacular defense, David Wells won easily, 7–2.

Then the Indians won game two, 4–1, in twelve innings. When they also won game three, 6–1, the Yankees appeared to be in deep trouble.

But Jeter demonstrated his leadership. After the game he was calm and confident. "You never like to lose," he said, "but it's a seven-game series. You have to win four games before you lose four games." In other words, this was no time for the Yankees to panic.

They didn't. Pitcher Orlando "El Duque" Hernandez mesmerized the Indians in game four and David Wells beat Cleveland handily in game five.

In the first inning of game six, after Chuck Knoblauch made an out, Jeter beat out an infield hit to end a 3 for 20 slump, then went to third when Paul O'Neill executed a perfect hit and run. Both eventually scored, and the Yankees jumped out to an early lead.

But the Indians refused to quit. They chipped away at the lead and entering the sixth inning trailed, 6–5.

With Joe Girardi and Scott Brosius on base, Jeter stepped in against Cleveland reliever Paul Shuey. Jeter explained later, "In that situation I just want to get a ball I can hit and drive it." That he did. Shuey hung a curveball and Jeter hit it to the gap, knocking in both Girardi and Brosius with a triple. The Indians' Omar Vizquel later called the hit "a knife in the heart." Relief pitchers Ramiro Mendoza and

Mariano Rivera shut Cleveland down the rest of the way, and the Yankees won, 9–5, to capture the American League pennant.

New York faced the surprising San Diego Padres in the World Series. But the Padres were doomed before they even came to the plate the first time. After coming back to beat Cleveland, the Yankees were unstoppable.

Jeter understood what playing in the World Series meant, describing it as "a Broadway play, center stage." He was ready for a starring role.

After falling behind in game one, 5–2, New York exploded against San Diego's ace pitcher Kevin Brown, scoring seven seventh-inning runs to win, 9–6. Then in game two Jeter went 2 for 5 and paced the Yankees to a 9–3 win.

The Padres fought hard in game three, but Scott Brosius hammered two home runs as the Yankees came back to win, 5–4, and lead the Series three games to none.

But San Diego was resilient. No team likes being swept, and in game four pitcher Kevin Brown seemed determined to make up for his game one defeat. Over the first five innings he held the Yankees scoreless. Fortunately, New York's Andy Pettitte similarly shut down the Padres.

In the sixth inning, Jeter came to bat. He fought off a tough pitch from Brown and chopped it into the ground toward third base.

Jeter broke out of the batter's box, running hard from his first step. Jeter was still following his parents' advice that "there's never any excuse for anyone to work harder than you do."

San Diego third baseman Ken Caminiti charged the ball, but Jeter beat the throw. Paul O'Neill then singled him to third and Bernie Williams beat out an infield hit to bring him in. New York led, 1–0.

That's all the Yankees needed. Jeter walked and scored a second run in the eighth inning, but when San Diego pinch hitter Mark Sweeney grounded to Scott Brosius with two out in the ninth, it was all over. Brosius fielded the ball cleanly and threw it to first base. The Yankees were world champions again. By winning the World Series they improved their season record to an amazing 125–50. Without question, the 1998 Yankees were one of the greatest teams in baseball history.

For the second time in three seasons the Yankees

were honored with a parade and a celebration at City Hall. When Jeter took the microphone, he knew exactly what to say. After all, he was getting to be an old hand at this kind of thing.

"I don't think there's a person in the world who's been more spoiled than I've been," he said. "I've had an opportunity to win two world championships in my first three years. I'm playing for the best manager, in the best city, for the best owner, in front of the best fans in the world. There was only one thing wrong with this season. We didn't get the opportunity to win the World Series at home.

"I guess we're going to have to come back and do it next year."

Chapter Eleven:

1999

Saving the Season

So much had gone right for Derek Jeter and the New York Yankees in 1998 that it didn't seem possible for things to get better in 1999. But Yankee owner George Steinbrenner is never satisfied.

Star pitcher Roger Clemens of the Toronto Blue Jays wanted to be traded. Clemens, who won five Cy Young Awards pitching for Boston and Toronto, had accomplished everything in his career but winning a world championship.

Steinbrenner had tried to acquire Clemens before. Now he seized the chance, sending the Jays popular pitcher David Wells and two other players for Clemens.

The deal shocked the baseball world. As incredible as it appeared, the Yankees seemed to be even better at the beginning of 1999 than they had been in 1998. But baseball and life have a way of evening things out. Just when the Yankees seemed absolutely unbeatable, a series of tragedies struck. First, Yankee Hall-of-Famer Joe DiMaggio, who many people considered the greatest all-around player in the history of the game, passed away. Then Darryl Strawberry, who was hoping to return after beating cancer, was arrested for possessing cocaine and was immediately suspended from baseball. And then, during a physical exam at the beginning of spring training, manager Joe Torre was diagnosed with prostate cancer. Fortunately, doctors caught the disease early, when it could still be treated, but Torre would have to miss spring training and the beginning of the season. Coach Don Zimmer took over.

Strawberry's arrest and Torre's health problems shook Derek Jeter. He was very close to Strawberry, who had taken a particular interest in the young star and warned him of the perils he might face. Strawberry's own career provided dramatic evidence of all that could go wrong. At one time he had seemed like a certain Hall-of-Famer. But he had succumbed to the temptations of fame and wasted much of his talent, becoming an alcoholic and cocaine addict. Now it appeared as if his addictions would cost him his career.

Jeter was similarly close to the man that he still called "Mr. Torre." Torre served as almost a surrogate father to Derek. On the rare occasions when Jeter made a mistake, he was usually so embarrassed he went to Torre and apologized before the manager even had a chance to say anything to him.

But Jeter was now beginning his fourth season in the major leagues. He knew he had to stay strong and lead by example.

During the off-season, he had taken the Yankees to arbitration for a new contract, earning a new deal worth over four million dollars for the season. At the arbitration hearing, the Yankees only complaint about his play concerned his power at the plate. Disappointed at hitting "only" 19 home runs in 1998, he'd worked out harder than ever before in the off-season and gotten stronger. On opening day Jeter went 3 for 3 with a home run.

Everyone noticed the change. Former Yankee great Reggie Jackson said Jeter now reminded him of a young Ken Griffey. Paul O'Neill added his praise by saying, "Derek is becoming the best player I've ever played with. That's how talented he is. He does whatever he needs to do, whatever the situation calls for, whether it's a base hit, moving a runner over, or hitting a home run. He's incredible."

Yet after a quick start, the Yankees got off stride. In mid-May the Boston Red Sox, the Yankees historical rivals, took over the lead in the American League East. Some people expected the Yankees to collapse.

But almost by himself, Derek Jeter kept that from happening. Over the first few months of the season, he led the league at one time or another in almost every hitting category — batting average, runs, on-base percentage, slugging percentage, and total bases — and was among the league leaders in home runs and RBIs. Incredibly, of his first 78 games, Jeter reached base in 76 of them. When Joe Torre finally returned, he temporarily moved Jeter from the number-two spot to the third position in the batting order to take advantage of his hot bat.

On June 26, Jeter celebrated his twenty-fifth birthday. Before the game against Baltimore, his teammates teased him for being so old. "I am getting old," joked Jeter. "I probably won't even be able to play the whole game." Everyone laughed.

But in the eighth inning, no one was laughing. With the Yankees leading, 3–1, Bernie Williams doubled. Jeter then came to bat and bounced a ball up the middle. As he crossed first base to beat out the infield hit, he grabbed the back of his left thigh and limped to a stop.

Yankee trainer Gene Monahan raced out onto the field. It appeared as if Jeter had pulled his hamstring, an injury that takes a long time to heal. Pitcher David Cone said later, "Everyone held their breath. He's the one guy we cannot afford to lose for an extended period of time."

Fortunately, the injury was just a cramp, not a pull. Nevertheless, manager Joe Torre removed him from the game. He didn't want to take any chances with the best player on the team.

Jeter returned to the lineup two days later and by midsummer the Yankees had resumed their place atop the American League East. In fan balloting for the All-Star Game, scheduled to be played in Boston, Jeter, leading the league in hitting, held a big lead over Red Sox shortstop Nomar Garciaparra. It appeared as if Jeter would be named the American League's starting All-Star shortstop for the first time.

But when the starting lineup was announced, Garciaparra had beat out Jeter by a few thousand votes. In the final week of voting, he'd somehow overcome an enormous deficit.

It was soon revealed how. The 1999 All-Star Game was the first in which fans were allowed to vote over the Internet. Some students at the Massachusetts Institute of Technology, a college near Boston, had figured out a way to vote for Garciaparra thousands of times.

Another player might have reacted angrily, but Jeter took his defeat magnanimously. Garciaparra was having a good year himself, and Jeter was much more concerned with team goals than any individual honors.

Yankee manager Joe Torre, who served as the American League manager, named Jeter to the team as a backup. When Jeter replaced Garciaparra in midgame, he showed the Boston fans that he had no hard feelings over the snub. Just the opposite.

When Jeter stepped into the batter's box, he performed an exaggerated imitation of Garciaparra, who before every pitch adjusts his batting gloves over and over again, then alternately taps the toe of each shoe into the ground. Jeter's antics made everyone laugh. Although Derek didn't get a hit, the A.L. won, 4–1.

At the end of July, with his batting average a league-high .369, Jeter went into a slump, his first of the season. For the next month he hit only .282. His batting average dropped by more than twenty points and Garciaparra took over the league lead.

Entering September, the Yankees retained a narrow lead over the Red Sox, who they just couldn't seem to shake in the division race. But just as it looked as if Boston might catch them, Jeter and the Yankees got hot again. Jeter hit .364 in the final month of the season, finishing with an average of .349, second to Garciaparra. The Yankees easily won the A.L. East to qualify for the playoffs.

After their spectacular performance in 1998, winning a divisional title wasn't very impressive. Many observers wrote that the Yankees didn't seem nearly as strong as in 1998. Only Jeter had a better year in 1999, with career highs of 24 home runs and 104 RBIs. Pitcher Roger Clemens had struggled in place of David Wells, and a number of other Yankees, such as Paul O'Neill, Scott Brosius, and Jorge

Posada simply didn't play as well in 1999 as they had in 1998. Critics complained that the Yankees had won "only" 98 games. Not many people expected the Yankees to make it back to the World Series again, much less win it.

But everyone underestimated New York's resolve. Winning 98 games was still an impressive achievement, and several key Yankees had been playing in spite of some personal tragedies. Chuck Knoblauch's father was ill with Alzheimer's disease, and late in the season Scott Brosius's father had died. The Yankees were determined to prove their critics wrong.

For the third time in four seasons, they faced the Texas Rangers in the first round of the playoffs. And for the third time in four seasons, New York's pitching made the Rangers look like Little Leaguers.

In the first game Orlando Hernandez held Texas to only two hits and the Yanks rolled to an 8–0 win. In game two Andy Pettitte pitched seven strong innings as New York won, 3–1.

The Yankees ended the series fast in game three. In the first inning Jeter started things off with a long triple to left field. Then Bernie Williams walked and Darryl Strawberry, who'd been allowed to return after serving his suspension, homered to put the Yankees ahead, 3–0. That's all the runs they needed, as Roger Clemens pitched New York to victory.

The win earned the Yankees the right to play the Red Sox for the pennant. Fans everywhere looked forward to the meeting between the two archrivals. It would give fans an opportunity to see Jeter and Garciaparra go head-to-head. Jeter dismissed talk of any rivalry between the two players, saying, "He's not pitching against me, and I'm not pitching against him."

Many observers thought Boston would win. Red Sox pitcher Pedro Martinez had been almost untouchable all year long and he'd overcome an injury to lead the Sox over Cleveland in the division playoffs.

Fortunately for the Yankees, Martinez needed to rest and wouldn't be able to pitch until game three. By then, the Red Sox already trailed, having crumbled against New York's superb pitching and having made too many mistakes in the field.

As usual Jeter was in the middle of everything. After committing an error in the first inning of game one to give the Sox a run, Jeter's seventh-inning single tied the game before Bernie Williams won it with a tenth-inning home run, 4–3. And in game two Jeter's airtight defense, walk, and base hit helped the Yankees to a 3–2 win.

As expected, Martinez beat the Yankees, 13–1, in game three, but Jeter collected one of New York's three hits. The Yankees still led the series two games to one.

In game four the Yankees led only 3–2 entering the ninth inning. But Knoblauch and Jeter started the inning with hits and the Yanks exploded for six runs to win, 9–2. One more victory would allow them to return to the World Series.

The Yankees knew that if they didn't win game five, they would face Pedro Martinez in game six. They didn't want to take any chances.

Knoblauch led off the game with a single and Jeter stepped in against Boston pitcher Kent Mercker. As the crowd at Boston's Fenway Park chanted, "No-mar's bet-ter!" Jeter was determined to get the Yankees off to a quick start.

Admitting later that he was "looking for a pitch to drive," he silenced the crowd with one swing, blasting a towering home run into the center field bleachers. New York led, 2–0, before the Red Sox came to bat.

The homer deflated the crowd and took them out of the ball game. The Red Sox fell apart and the Yankees won, 6–1. It would be the Yankees facing the Braves in a rematch of the 1996 World Series.

Perhaps this time, as Jeter had hoped for almost a year earlier, they could win the World Series in New York. Now they had a chance to make Jeter's prediction come true.

Chapter Twelve:
1999

A Champion Again

People were starting to realize that perhaps the 1999 Yankees were just as good as their 1998 counterparts after all. And Derek Jeter was one of the big reasons why. So far, he'd gotten a hit in every game of the postseason. In the big matchup against the Red Sox and Nomar Garciaparra, Jeter had come out on top. Although Garciaparra had cracked two home runs to Jeter's one and out-hit Jeter .400 to .350, the Red Sox star had also made four costly errors. Jeter's two errors had been relatively insignificant, and his leadoff home run in game five had been huge. Of the two players, Boston manager Jimy Williams accurately said, "They exemplify what a lot of ballplayers wish they were."

The World Series opened in Atlanta with Braves ace Greg Maddux squaring off against Orlando Hernandez, who in two seasons had yet to lose in post-season play. Entering the eighth inning, the Braves led, 1–0, and were only six outs away from victory.

But the Yankees fought back and loaded the bases, bringing up Derek Jeter. He quickly fouled off two pitches to fall behind in the count.

Crafty Greg Maddux is one of the best pitchers in baseball history. He tries to get ahead of batters and make them overanxious. His remarkable control often forces hitters to swing at pitches just off the plate.

That is precisely what he tried to get Jeter to do. A year or two before, Jeter likely would have swung at the pitch, but he'd since learned to be more patient. He leaned over the plate and watched the close pitch sail past for ball one.

Maddux reacted angrily. Now he had to throw a strike.

Jeter jumped at the pitch and slapped it into left field for a single. Scott Brosius scored easily. The game was tied!

The hit unnerved Maddux. Suddenly, he started missing with his pitches. The Yankees went on to score three more runs to win the game, 4–1.

Of game two, Jeter said later, "We wanted to get

ahead early and take the crowd out of the game." They did precisely that.

Chuck Knoblauch performed his job of leadoff hitter to perfection and started the game with a single off Atlanta's Kevin Millwood. Then Jeter followed with another hit. Within moments, the Yankees had scored three runs off the struggling pitcher. Then, in the fourth, Jeter doubled and scored. New York pitcher David Cone cruised to the 7–2 win.

The two teams traveled to New York for game three. In 1996, the Yankees had lost their first two games at home only to go to Atlanta and sweep the Braves. Now the Braves hoped to do the same to New York.

At first it appeared as if they might be successful. Atlanta jumped ahead and led, 5–2, entering the seventh inning.

But the Yankees remained patient against Atlanta starter Tom Glavine. Tino Martinez homered to make the score 5–3, and in the eighth inning Chuck Knoblauch hit a home run that barely cleared the fence in right field to tie the game. New York's bullpen ace Mariano Rivera held Atlanta at bay, and when Chad Curtis homered in the tenth the Yankees took a commanding three games to none lead in the Series.

The Braves knew that no team in baseball history had ever won the Series after losing the first three games, but they didn't give up. They sent ace pitcher John Smoltz to the mound in game four before a raucous crowd in Yankee Stadium to try to start their comeback.

The Yankees were determined not to let that happen, but not just because they wanted to win. Before the game right fielder Paul O'Neill learned that his father had died. He insisted on playing. Jeter and the other Yankees knew that O'Neill needed to be with his family. They wanted to end the Series as quickly as possible.

In the third inning, with the game scoreless, Chuck Knoblauch led off with an infield single. Jeter stepped up to the plate and looked carefully at third base coach Willie Randolph. Randolph flashed him the hit-and-run sign.

The pitch came in and Jeter served it softly into right field. Perfect! Knoblauch, running on the pitch, went to third on the hit.

With Paul O'Neill at the plate, Jeter watched

Smoltz carefully. With two strikes on O'Neill, Jeter bolted for second base.

O'Neill struck out, but Jeter slid in safely to get into scoring position. When Bernie Williams walked and Tino Martinez and Jorge Posada followed with singles, the Yankees led, 3–0.

Meanwhile Roger Clemens responded with one of his best games of the year. With a 3–1 lead in the eighth he turned the game over to the Yankee bullpen. Closer Mariano Rivera hadn't been scored upon since late July, and he dominated the Braves. Jim Leyritz socked a home run in the bottom of the eighth to increase the Yankee lead to 4–1. When Keith Lockhart lofted a fly ball to left field with two outs in the ninth, Chad Curtis circled under it to make the catch and make the Yankees world champions.

Jeter rushed in from shortstop to join his teammates in a brief celebration at the mound, but it was subdued, for the Yankees knew that Paul O'Neill was in mourning. They huddled around him and dashed into the clubhouse.

Meanwhile the crowd at Yankee Stadium stood and cheered, calling the Yankees back out onto the field again and again to make curtain calls. Just as Jeter had hoped, this year the Yanks had won the World Series in New York. When he came back out of the clubhouse, he stood on the dugout and sprayed his fans with champagne.

Before Derek Jeter joined the New York Yankees, the team hadn't won a World Series in sixteen long seasons. But in the first four years that he lived out his dream as Yankee shortstop, they won three championships. "I don't think you ever take them for granted," he said.

As manager Joe Torre said of Jeter after the 2000 Series, "Three world championships in four seasons? That's kind of like a dream, isn't it?"

But for Derek Jeter, the dream still wasn't over.

Chapter Thirteen:
2000–2003

Dream On

After the Yankees won the 1999 World Series, many people expected the team to struggle in 2000. After all, every member of the starting lineup except Jeter and catcher Jorge Posada was over thirty years old, and older players sometimes get hurt or start to slow down a bit.

But Jeter and the Yankees got off to a quick start. The star shortstop reached base in 25 of his first 26 games, and the Yankees started the season 22–9. A 100-win season and another world championship suddenly seemed likely.

Then, slowly at first, everything started falling apart. In late May Jeter pulled a hamstring muscle while running the bases, and he missed more than two weeks. The Yankees went into a mild slump. The slump grew worse after Roger Clemens pulled a groin muscle. Ace pitcher David Cone struggled on the mound. Jeter returned to the lineup in June and worked his way to an impressive .371, but no one else was having as good a year — and one man's performance wasn't enough to keep the team in the lead. As Boston and Toronto briefly pulled ahead of New York, one major league scout commented of the Yankees, "They don't look special anymore."

The only team that looked special was the Yankees' crosstown rival, the New York Mets. Paced by starting catcher Mike Piazza, the Mets suddenly appeared to be the best bet to win a world championship in 2000.

But just before the All-Star break, the Yankees made their move. First they traded for Indian slugger David Justice. Then, Roger Clemens came off the disabled list. The Yankees swept the Mets in a hotly contested three-game series to vault into first place at the All-Star break.

For the third time in his career, Jeter was named to the All-Star Team. Starting shortstop Alex Rodriguez of the Mariners was injured, so All-Star manager Joe Torre picked Jeter to start the game at shortstop. Jeter was thrilled, and it showed in his play. He fielded flawlessly and cracked a key two-run double to lead the American League to victory, earning him All-Star MVP honors, the first Yankee ever to win the award.

Behind Jeter, the Yankees surged in the second half of the season, and with only nineteen games left they led the division by nine games. Then, all of a sudden, they couldn't win, going a terrible 3–16 over the remainder of the season.

Fortunately, they managed to hang on for the division title with a record of 87–74. But of all the teams that qualified for post-season play, the Yankees had the worst regular-season record. After they lost their first two playoff games to the Oakland A's, it appeared as if New York's season was about to end. If Oakland won one more game, the Yankees were done.

But Jeter and his teammates didn't quit. They came back to beat Oakland in three straight games and then thumped the Seattle Mariners to reach the World Series once again. Meanwhile, in the National League, the New York Mets won the pennant and the right to play the Yankees. It was the first time that the two New York teams had met in the

World Series since 1956. The so-called "Subway Series" had the whole city of New York going crazy with anticipation.

Game one at the Mets' Shea Stadium was a closely fought contest as Andy Pettitte went up against Met pitcher Al Leiter. In the sixth inning the score was still tied at 0–0. Then the Mets threatened to break the game open. Rookie Timo Perez reached first base and Todd Zeile drove the ball to deep left field. Zeile was certain he had hit a home run and left the batter's box in a home run trot. Perez thought the hit was a home run, too. He raised his arm in celebration and started a slow jog around the bases ahead of Zeile.

But the ball fell inches short of a home run, hitting off the top of the left field wall. Yankee fans started to roar while Met fans sank back in their seats. Zeile and Perez, one of the fastest runners in the league, suddenly started running hard as Yankee outfielder David Justice fielded the carom. But his throw toward the infield was wild and, despite Perez's late start, the Yankees didn't appear to have a chance to throw him out at home.

No one told *that* to Derek Jeter. As he saw

Justice's throw sail toward the foul line in short right field, he sprinted after the ball and caught it on a dead run. Then, in one fluid motion, he spun and threw toward home as if he was fielding a ground ball deep in the hole behind shortstop. The ball landed just short of the plate and then bounced perfectly into Jorge Posada's glove. He applied the tag to the sliding Perez. A split second later, the umpire signaled "Out!"

Jeter pumped his fist and Yankee fans roared. They believed there was no other player in the game who could have made the play.

The Yankees fought off the Mets to win the game in extra innings. Over the next five games, every time the Mets seemed about to get back into the Series, Jeter stopped them, finding himself in the middle of almost every Yankee rally. The Yankees won the World Series in six games. Jeter, with a .409 batting average, was named Series MVP. He became the first player ever to be named MVP of both the All-Star Game and the World Series in the same season. Then again, there aren't many players like Derek Jeter. In his first five big league seasons, he now had four world championship rings!

At the season's end, Jeter's contract was up. Yankee management wanted their talented and popular player to remain with the team. They knew that Jeter was a special player on and off the field. So before the start of spring training, they signed him to a ten-year contract worth an incredible 180 million dollars!

Unfortunately, Jeter missed the start of the 2001 season with a pulled muscle. For much of the first half of the season, New York trailed its arch rival, the Boston Red Sox, for first place. In early September, however, the Yankees beat the Red Sox in the first three games of a four-game series to pull ahead. The final game, scheduled for September 10, 2001, was rained out.

The next morning, September 11, was absolutely beautiful. The skies cleared and the sun shone brightly. That night, pitcher Roger Clemens was scheduled to try for his fifteenth win in a row and twentieth of the season. The Yankees were finally starting to think about the post-season.

Then, shortly before nine o'clock, horrific events occurred that changed everything. Two airplanes hijacked by terrorists smashed into the "Twin Towers" of the World Trade Center, New York's tallest buildings. Hundreds of people were instantly killed, and when both buildings collapsed a few hours later, more than two thousand more people died, including hundreds of police officers and firemen who were trying to rescue people. Another plane dive-bombed the Pentagon in Washington, killing hundreds more. A fourth was downed by courageous passengers who overtook the hijackers, sacrificing their own lives to keep the terrorists from flying to their target.

As shockwaves from the attacks reverberated around the world, the entire country went on alert. Everyday life came to a standstill. The baseball season was suspended indefinitely.

But suddenly, baseball didn't seem very important — not even to Jeter or any of his teammates. They knew that playing a game was insignificant compared to the work of the rescuers at what became known as "Ground Zero," the site of the World Trade Center tragedy. Like almost everyone else in New York, Yankee players spent the first day or so trying to locate their friends and families to make sure they were okay. Jeter, who lives in Manhattan, let his parents know he was safe. Then, like so many other people in the world, he watched television coverage of the tragedy in horror. He couldn't believe it.

The New York Yankees did all they could to help those who were suffering. Jeter and his teammates spent time visiting with the families of the victims, giving them hugs and letting them know that they cared about what had just happened. Jeter admitted, "There is no way us coming out here can help heal this city or this country." But he also knew that, even if for a moment, "it makes people feel better."

At its best, a sport provides relief from our day-to-day struggles in life. New York City was struggling like it never had before as the entire city mourned. When the baseball season resumed on September 18, the Yankees hoped to provide a few hours of distraction each day. This, they felt, would be the best way they could help their city begin to heal.

Even so, Jeter and his teammates found it hard to concentrate on baseball. No one knew if New York would be attacked again, and the Yankees — and Yankee Stadium — were very visible targets. Every game was played under tight security. Despite this stress, however, the Yankees still managed to end the regular season in first place.

When the playoffs began, the Yankees played poorly and lost the first two games to the Oakland Athletics in New York. No one on the team except Jeter was playing very well. The Yankees looked exhausted. No one expected them to bounce back.

In game three Yankee pitcher Mike Mussina, who had been signed as a free agent in the off-season, managed to focus on the game and pitch shutout ball. Entering the seventh inning, the Yankees led 1–0. Then the A's broke through. With two outs Jeremy Giambi singled. Then Terence Long hit a double into the left field corner.

Shane Spencer of the Yankees corralled the ball and threw home in a desperate attempt to get Giambi. But his throw sailed over the heads of both cutoff men, second baseman Alfonso Soriano and first baseman Tino Martinez. As it did, the Yankees' hope for another world championship seemed about to disappear.

Then, out of nowhere, came Derek Jeter! Like some kind of superhero swooping in to save the day, he rocketed in from his shortstop position all the way across the diamond. He caught the throw on a dead run and tumbled into foul territory in front of the dugout. Then, without stopping or even slowing down, he flipped a backhanded shovel pass to catcher Jorge Posada. A shocked Giambi, who seconds ago thought he would score easily, didn't even bother to slide. Posada slapped a tag on Giambi's leg a split second before he touched the plate. Out!

No one anywhere, *ever,* had seen a more heads-up play. Many called it the greatest defensive play in the history of baseball. As Yankee third baseman Scott Brosius said later, "You just don't practice the old run-toward-the-dugout-and-make-a-backhand-flip-to-the-catcher play." That is, unless you are Derek Jeter. He had been dreaming of making such plays since he was a little boy. "I was where I was supposed to be," he said matter-of-factly.

The miracle play sent the A's reeling and made New Yorkers cheer again. The Yankees won the game and the series, and then went on to dump the Mariners, winners of 116 regular season games, to reach the World Series once again. By now, the Yankees had captured the hearts of the whole nation.

But the Arizona Diamondbacks, National League

champs, had Randy Johnson and Curt Schilling, two of the best pitchers in the game. And after they beat the Yankees in the first two games, it seemed as if Jeter's dream of another world championship was over. Still, New York fought back valiantly, winning game three.

Then, in game four, the Yankees trailed with two outs in the ninth when Tino Martinez tied it with a home run. The score was still tied when Jeter stepped to the plate in the tenth inning. He had hurt his shoulder tumbling into the stands to make a great catch against Oakland and hadn't hit well since. Then, all of a sudden . . .

Home run! Jeter drove the ball over the fence to win the game and tie the Series!

Incredibly, the Yankees won game five in another stirring comeback to take command of the series.

But not even Derek Jeter's dreams come true all the time. The Diamondbacks surged back to win game six and then take the Series with a rousing come-from-behind victory of their own in game seven. Still, Jeter and his teammates had provided the nation with a wonderful, thrilling break from the recent tragedy.

Since 2001, Jeter and the Yankees have been trying to return to the World Series. In 2002, they won the Eastern Division title again, and Jeter hit .500 with two home runs in the division series. But the Yankees lost to the eventual world champions, the Anaheim Angels.

Derek Jeter doesn't like to lose, but he also knows that it takes hard work to live your dream, and he still has goals he wants to accomplish. In the 2003 season, Yankee owner George Steinbrenner recognized him as a team leader and named Jeter the Yankee captain, the first captain since the death of Thurmon Munson in 1979.

Chapter Fourteen:
2004-2007

Captain Jeter

Steinbrenner's June 3rd announcement coincided with Jeter's return to the lineup after a six-week stint on the disabled list for a dislocated shoulder. The injury had occurred on Opening Day in April, when Jeter had collided with Toronto Blue Jays catcher Ken Huckaby while sliding headfirst into third base.

Unfortunately for Jeter, the dislocated shoulder was just one of three injuries he would suffer in 2003. A few weeks after he was named captain, a hard-thrown pitch struck his wrist. The wrist wasn't broken, but it did keep him out of play for another week. And then, toward the end of the season, Jeter strained a rib muscle and wound up on the disabled list yet again.

Despite these setbacks, Jeter and the Yankees battled their way to the World Series once again. But any hope Jeter had of adding a fifth ring was dashed by the Florida Marlins. In game one, Florida beat New York 3–2 in Yankee Stadium, the first time the Yankees had been bested in their home town in the World Series since 1996. Five games later, the Marlins had won three more to take the Series.

In the wake of the loss, George Steinbrenner decided it was time to add some more muscle to the lineup. He set his sights on Texas Ranger shortstop Alex "A-Rod" Rodriguez—and got him.

There was just one problem: Derek Jeter was the Yankees' shortstop. A-Rod and Jeter had been friends for years, but now there were wild rumors that the two weren't on speaking terms. The rumors only ended when it was announced that Rodriguez would be playing third base, not shortstop.

"I am Derek's biggest fan," Rodriguez once said. "I would give him the shirt off my back if he needed it."

But at the start of the 2004 season, it wasn't a shirt Jeter needed, it was a hit. In the first weeks, he came to bat thirty-two times in a row, only to return to the dugout each time without a hit.

Many players would lose their cool in the midst of such a slump. But Jeter remained calm, noting that everyone has bad days and that throwing a fit on the field wasn't going to change that fact. Only hard work and focus would. On April 29, his hard work and focus paid off when he smashed a slump-ending home run before thousands of cheering fans in Yankee Stadium.

Still, the hitless streak did raise many eyebrows in the baseball community. Perhaps Jeter was affected by A-Rod after all; or maybe he was just starting to slide, as so many other superstar players had.

Jeter dispelled these doubts on July 1. New York was hosting Boston in a 3–3 game that seemed to have no end. In the top of the twelfth inning, the Sox put runners on second and third with two outs. A hit now could load the bases or even give Boston the winning run. An out would give New York another chance to beat their rivals.

Trot Nixon came up to bat. He boosted a pop fly down the left field line.

Jeter ran full tilt, glove outstretched. He nabbed the ball in a fabulous over-the-shoulder catch close to the foul line—and had such a head of steam going that he had to dive into the stands or else crash into the barrier!

When Jeter stood up, his face was bloody but the ball was still nestled in his glove. Nixon was out, the inning was over, and the Yankees went on to win the game in thirteen innings. The catch, later known as The Dive, was voted Play of the Year by Major League Baseball fans, and proved once again how dedicated and determined Jeter was to give his all.

With plays like that from Jeter and the rest of the squad, the Yankees made it into the postseason once more. And then, in the ALCS against the Red Sox, New York made it into the record books. Unfortunately, it was a record they would have been much happier without.

The Yankees were up in the seven game series 3–0. It seemed a sure thing that they would advance to the World Series. After all, they only had to win one more game.

Instead, they lost four in a row! No team in the history of baseball had ever given up a three game advantage in the postseason. The Red Sox went on to become the World Series champs; the Yankees went home with their tails between their legs.

While many in the baseball community tried to analyze where New York had gone wrong, Jeter had a simple explanation for the loss. "They played better than us. That's basically it," he said in an interview. "You can come up with this or that, but the bottom line is that they beat us."

In the off-season, George Steinbrenner went shopping for new players yet again. This time, he came back with three pitchers, including star hurler Randy Johnson. But as strong as the bullpen was on paper, on the mound the pitchers struggled for consistency. It was up to the rest of the team to make up the difference.

Derek Jeter did his part, of course, and added a few personal firsts while doing so. Two days after posting his ninth Opening Day start at shortstop, he powered in a walk-off home run against the Red Sox. A month later, he had lead-off hits in five consecutive games, a personal career best. The following month, he went to the plate thirty-four times without a strikeout, his longest streak since 2002.

But the highlight of the first half of his season came on June 18 in a game against the Chicago Cubs. It was the top of the sixth inning. The bases were loaded. Jeter came up to bat.

In similar situations in the past, Jeter often batted at least one runner in. Sometimes he made an out. But never, in the 136 times he'd come to bat with the bases loaded, had he blasted a grand-slam homer.

This time, however, he did—a clear shot into left center field for his first ever grand slam home run!

"I never thought I'd hit one," he said happily after the game. "I'd be lying to you if I said I didn't feel good right now."

Jeter and the Yankees played well enough to earn a berth in the postseason yet again. But that year, they only lasted one round, bowing out after three losses to the Los Angeles Angels.

"We had our chances up until the last inning, but we fell short, " Jeter said after their third defeat. "It's not an easy thing to do. If it was easy to do, a lot of teams would be doing it. You have to be the hottest team, and we haven't been the hottest team the last few years."

The last five years, to be exact, for the Yankees hadn't reached the World Series since 2000. Many wondered if they would do it the next year, or if once again they would suffer in the postseason.

If they did, it wasn't for lack of trying on the part of the team's captain. In 2006, Derek Jeter had one of his best seasons ever. His batting average of .343 was the second best in the American League. That average, together with his ninety-plus RBIs and thirty-plus steals, made him only one of five players in the last seventy-five years to post such high numbers in a single season.

He also had more than 200 hits in 2006, the fifth season he'd passed that benchmark. In Yankee history, only Lou Gehrig had done the same thing; in MLB history, no other shortstop had reached that milestone.

Still, no statistic mattered to Jeter as much as helping his team to reach and win the World Series. But for the sixth year in a row, despite having the best record in the American League, the championship of the baseball world would elude the Yankees. They fell short early on, losing the Division Series 3-1 to the surprisingly sharp-clawed Detroit Tigers.

The Yankees performed well the following year, earning a wild card slot in the playoffs with a regular season record of 94 wins and 68 losses. Jeter was a big part of their success. Defensively, he ended with a new personal best of 104 double plays. His offensive prowess won him his eighth trip to the All-Star game, the 2007 ESPY Best Ballplayer award, and his second consecutive Silver Slugger award. For the third season in a row and the sixth of his career, he connected for more than 200 hits to finish with an average of .322.

Unfortunately, in the postseason his bat fell nearly silent. In the Yankees' first division series game against the Cleveland Indians, he popped out, struck out, flied out, and lined out. New York lost game one of the five-game series, 12–3.

Neither team did much hitting in game two. By the bottom of the eighth the score stood at New York 1, Cleveland 0. The Yankees hoped to hold the Indians scoreless for two more innings to even up the series.

But it wasn't to be, for suddenly, out of nowhere, massive clouds of tiny flying insects swarmed the players! Yankee reliever Joba Chamberlain tried to ignore the bugs crawling into his ears, nose, eyes, and mouth, but couldn't. His pitching turned wild and by inning's end, the Indians had knotted the score.

The Bug Game, as the match was later dubbed, went into extra innings. New York failed to get on base. Cleveland, meanwhile, scored again in the bottom of the eleventh to take it 2–1. They now were up in the series, 2–0.

The Yankees fought their way halfway out of the hole in game three, trouncing the Indians 8–4. That was their final victory of the year, however. Game four saw Cleveland hold off a late surge by New York to win 6–4 and capture the division title.

Jeter had gone just 3-for-17 for a dismal average of .176. While he was bitterly disappointed in his own performance and the fact that the Yankees were out of the postseason, he gave credit where credit was due.

"They deserved to move on," he said of the Indians, citing Cleveland's pitchers in particular.

Also moving on was someone Jeter called "a friend for life." Yankee manager Joe Torre was leaving the franchise for the Los Angeles Dodgers.

Jeter was sad to see his longtime mentor depart. "There has been no bigger influence on my professional development," he said of Torre.

Still, as team captain, he knew he didn't have time to dwell on his friend's departure. The next season would soon be upon him—and he had to get ready.

Chapter Fifteen:
2008-2009

Chasing Gehrig

Any concern Derek Jeter had with the change in management vanished when Joe Girardi, a one-time Yankee player, accepted the position of team manager. "I'm already comfortable with him," Jeter told the press during spring training.

With that hurdle behind him, Jeter looked ahead to the upcoming season. On April 1, he took the field for his twelfth start at shortstop; only Hall of Famer Phil Rizzuto had more opening day starts for the team. Jeter knocked in a single that game, a New York win over Toronto.

He added four more hits in the week that followed. Then, in a match against the Tampa Bay Rays, he was forced to the sidelines with a severe leg strain that had him on the bench for the next six games.

When he returned to the lineup, the Yankees

were midway through an extended road trip. They had played in Kansas City and then Boston and now, with their record at 6 wins, 7 losses, they were heading south to face Tampa Bay.

In his first game back, Jeter helped his team to a win by knocking in 2 RBIs in 5 at-bats. He upped his stats with solid performances the next two games as well, going a total of 5-for-8 at the plate with 3 RBIs and 3 runs scored.

But while Jeter was going strong, the team overall was stalling. By the end of the month, their record was 14–15; May saw them finish just one game above the .500 mark. That same month also found Jeter nursing a painful wrist injury caused by a hard-thrown pitch. He didn't miss any games, but his batting suffered.

The team suffered, too. At the All-Star break in mid-July, they were in third place in the AL East, a full seven games behind the first-place Boston Red Sox and five behind Tampa Bay. The Rays and the Sox swapped positions in August and by the conclusion of the regular season, Tampa Bay had clinched first place in the division, with Boston running a close second for the wild card playoff slot.

New York, meanwhile, was through. It was the first time since 1993 that they had failed to make it into the postseason.

"It basically boils down to we weren't good enough," Jeter said in the final week. "It's a huge disappointment."

Jeter's year-end stats were off, too, due in part to his injuries. While he still received his third Silver Slugger award, for the first time since 2004 he had fewer than 200 hits, with just 179. His batting average dipped as well, from .322 in 2007 to .300.

The end of the 2008 season also marked the end of an era that had lasted eighty-three years. World-famous Yankee Stadium, "The House That Ruth Built," was scheduled to be torn down. From now on, the team would play in a brand-new, state-of-the-art arena, also called Yankee Stadium, across the street.

"The last game [at the old Stadium] was pretty special," Jeter recalled in an interview later. "The fans were outstanding. . . . It's something that all of us will definitely remember."

And his reaction when asked about the upcoming 2009 season? "It's World Series or bust."

During the off-season, New York's front office did everything it could to make a 2009 World Series a reality for the Yankees. Besides their new stadium, they added pitching power with hurlers Carston Charles "CC" Sabathia and A. J. Burnett and acquired first baseman Mark Teixeira, among other roster changes. While the team was handed a setback when superstar third baseman Alex Rodriguez underwent hip surgery, sidelining him for the first months of the season, overall the Yankees promised to deliver a strong season.

Derek Jeter helped them live up to that promise. In the very first game in April, he came to bat 5 times and connected for 3 hits. By the end of the month, he had added 24 more hits, contributing a total of 14 runs.

The Yankees finished April with a record of 12 wins, 10 losses—good, but not good enough. They entered May in third place, behind the Boston Red Sox and the Toronto Blue Jays.

Those same three teams had slots one, two, and

three in the standings at the end of May, too, but the order was different. With 29 wins and 20 losses, New York was now at the top of the list. They were playing outstanding ball; in fact, on June 1, they set a new league record by completing their eighteenth consecutive game without an error.

That game, a 5–2 victory over the Cleveland Indians, saw Jeter leading off the first inning with a single to left. Later, he reached first on a bunt that put teammate Brett Gardner in scoring position. With those two hits, Jeter extended his hitting streak to fifteen consecutive games. He also joined Major League greats Hank Aaron, Stan Musial, and Al Simmons as just one of four players to collect 2,600 hits, 200 homers, and 1,000 RBIs in fifteen seasons.

And he just kept going. Throughout most of June and July, his batting average was at or above .300. On July 24, he slugged his 2,655th hit to vault over Hall of Fame hitting great Ted Williams into sixty-eigth place. Three weeks later, he had hit number 2,674—and the number one spot as the Major League's top-hitting shortstop.

"It's still kind of hard to believe, to say the least,"

Jeter said of achieving that record.

What wasn't hard to believe was that the Yankees were in first place in the AL East. Ever since the All-Star break, they had demolished nearly every team they met. How good were they? Out of thirty-one games played from July 17 to August 17, they lost only eight!

Jeter was equally amazing. For August alone, he had an astonishing 46 hits in 122 at bats for a monthly average of .377! And on September 11, he made history.

More than seventy years earlier, Lou Gehrig swung his mighty bat and connected for his 2,721st career hit, the most of any Yankee ever. Jeter had tied that number on September 9.

Now, in the bottom of the third inning of a rainy home game against the Baltimore Orioles, Derek Jeter stood in the batter's box. He let two pitches go by for balls. The third pitch looked good. He swung.

Pow! A sizzling grounder to right! Jeter sprinted down the baseline. Hit number 2,722, one more than Gehrig!

All play stopped as Jeter, grinning ear-to-ear,

threw his arms out wide and jogged back to the bag. His teammates stormed onto the field to surround him with congratulatory hugs and slaps on the back. Fans in the stands went wild, chanting "De-rek! Je-ter!" for more than three minutes. George Steinbrenner sent the following message: "For those who say today's game can't produce legendary players, I have two words: Derek Jeter."

The one sour note of the day was that the game ended in a 10–4 loss. But by that time, the Yankees had clinched their spot in the playoffs. On October 4, they ended the 162-game season with their 103rd win. Their record was the best of any major league team, and the best they had posted since 2002. Back then, they had been bounced out of the postseason when they lost the League Division Series to the Anaheim Angels. This year, everyone expected they would advance further.

But how much further would they go?

Chapter Sixteen:
2009-2010

Serious about the World Series

The Yankees' road to the World Series was paved with obstacles big and small. The first was the Minnesota Twins. The Twins and the Yankees had met seven times in the regular season. All seven had ended in defeat for Minnesota. Now New York made it an even ten by rolling over the Twins in three straight games to take the ALDS.

The next bump in the road was Los Angeles. Game one went to New York. So did game two, an exhausting five-hour, thirteen-inning match that ended at one o'clock in the morning! The third meeting was almost as long, but this time, the Angels defeated the Yankees 5–4 in eleven innings.

That win gave Los Angeles fans hope that their team might come out ahead of New York in the long run. Their hopes were put on hold when the Yankees crushed them 10–1 the next night, but rose again when the Angels flew higher than their opponent, 7–6, in game five.

A third win never came for Los Angeles, however. Instead, New York walked away with yet another victory. After failing to reach the postseason the year before, the Yankees were now on their way to their fortieth World Series!

"We want to enjoy this tonight," a quiet but happy Jeter told the press after the win. "We'll worry about Philly tomorrow."

The Philadelphia Phillies were worth worrying about. In May, they had beaten the Yankees twice in Yankee Stadium. On October 28, they made it three times, trouncing New York 6–1. Jeter had done his best to boost the team, connecting for a double and two singles in four at bats, but no player, no matter how good, can win a game alone.

Derek Jeter took to the field prior to game two, but not to warm up. That day he was presented with the Roberto Clemente award, given to a Major League player who has dedicated himself to helping his community. Jeter had been doing just that since he first created his Turn 2 Foundation, an organization devoted to getting kids to make healthy choices instead of using drugs and alcohol, in 1996.

"People in our position, they should take advantage of it," Jeter stated matter-of-factly. "They should try to give back as much as possible."

When the ceremony ended, game two began. It was a pitchers' duel between the Yankees' A. J. Burnett and the Phillies' Pedro Martinez, but after a long-fought battle, Burnett came out the winner. In seven innings, he allowed just 4 hits and struck out 9, compared to the 6 hits and 8 strikeouts for Martinez. One of those hits was a two-bagger from Jeter's bat, his sixteenth hit of the postseason.

With New York's victory, the Series was tied at one game each. Two nights later, Yankee fans celebrated both Halloween and another win for their team—and the celebration continued after the next game, when New York drew within one of capturing their twenty-seventh championship title. Alex Rodriguez was the big hero that day, blasting a double that scored Johnny Damon and broke the 4–4 ninth-inning tie. Jeter had contributed earlier, with a leadoff single to start the game, followed by a sprint to home to score the first run. He also added an RBI single in the fifth inning that put the Yankees ahead, 3–2.

One more game. That's all New York needed to win the World Series. They didn't get it on November 2, although they came close. The Phillies had an 8–2 lead going into the eighth inning, a lead they watched slowly shrink when Rodriguez hit a 2-run RBI double and then scored on a sacrifice. It shrank even more when Jorge Posada reached home after Jeter grounded out into a double play.

But in the end, the score stayed in Philadelphia's favor, 8–6. The Series returned to New York. At the November 4 game the teams were scoreless in the first inning, but then New York got two runs in the bottom of the second. Philadelphia answered soon after to make it 2–1.

Two innings later, Brett Gardner struck out, but Jeter singled to center. He got a free ride to second when Johnny Damon drew the walk—and cruised on to third when Mark Teixeira was hit by a pitch.

Bases loaded, one out. Rodriguez came up to bat but struck out swinging. Now designated hitter

Hideki Matsui strode into the batter's box. Matsui had had an on-again, off-again year at the plate, but had been more consistent in the postseason.

In this game, he wasn't consistent—he was incredible. His home run in the second inning had given the Yankees their two runs. This time up, he collected two strikes before sending the ball soaring for a 2-RBI single.

The score now read Yankees 4, Phillies 1. It stayed that way until the bottom of the fifth. Jeter led off with a ground rule double and reached third on a sacrifice. When Teixeira singled, Jeter took off for home—and made it!

Yankees 5, Phillies 1, but not for long. Matsui came up to bat once more. Once more, he drilled a 2-run hit!

Philadelphia managed to score 2 more runs, but that was all. Final score at the top of the ninth inning: New York 7, Philadelphia 3. Final game score of the 2009 World Series? Yankees 4, Philadelphia 2!

"It feels better than I remember it, man," Jeter said happily of their hard-won victory. "It's been a long time."

Chapter Seventeen:
2010 and Beyond

No Slowing Down!

Derek Jeter now had his fifth World Championship ring, his first since being named captain of the Yankees. It was a suitable ending to his remarkable season. After faltering a bit in 2008, he rebounded in 2009 to post his best stats in recent years. His batting average was up from .300 to .334, and he surpassed the 200-hits mark for the seventh time in his career with a total of 212 for the regular season. He received his fourth Gold Glove and Silver Slugger awards, as well as his second Hank Aaron award. He was also named *Sports Illustrated* Sportsman of the Year, the first Yankee to ever receive that honor.

And Derek Jeter isn't finished yet—not by a long shot. His sixteenth year in pinstripes will surely be one marked by more record-breaking milestones. He's already made that rarest of hits, an inside-the-park home run, and edged past Babe Ruth's 2,873 hit total to climb to the thirty-eighth slot on the all-time hit list.

"Anytime you get a chance to pass [Ruth] in anything, it's pretty special," he acknowledged.

"Pretty special" is how many people describe Derek Jeter. Others have used more exuberant language to praise the steady leadership and skill he brings to the diamond each and every game. His work off the field has also earned him the respect of his peers and the devotion of his fans and the children whose lives he's touched through his Turn 2 Foundation.

Take, for example, Jeter's reaction to something he learned from his sister, Sharlee. Sharlee had organized a team of kids to play baseball in an inner-city youth league. Unfortunately, the team hadn't scored a single run all season.

Some celebrity sports stars might not have given the matter another thought. But Jeter isn't like other celebrity sports stars. So when he had the chance, he spent an off-day coaching the team. His advice must have been good, because that day the squad posted a 1 on the scoreboard instead of their usual goose egg.

"They didn't win the game," Sharlee Jeter said, "but with that run scored, you would have thought they won the World Series."

With such hands-on dedication, it's no surprise that Jeter was named *USA Weekend*'s 2010 Most Caring Athlete. "Jeter is as good a person as he is a player," enthused Yankee Hall of Fame pitcher and Turn 2 spokesman Rich "Goose" Gossage. "He is my favorite player in the Major Leagues."

Most likely, Gossage—and countless other fans— will have plenty of years to watch and admire Derek Jeter, for Jeter intends to stay right where he is.

"I have the greatest job in the world," the Yankees' captain once said. "My dreams and my future lie in Yankee Stadium.

"I hope I wear this jersey forever."